AF605239

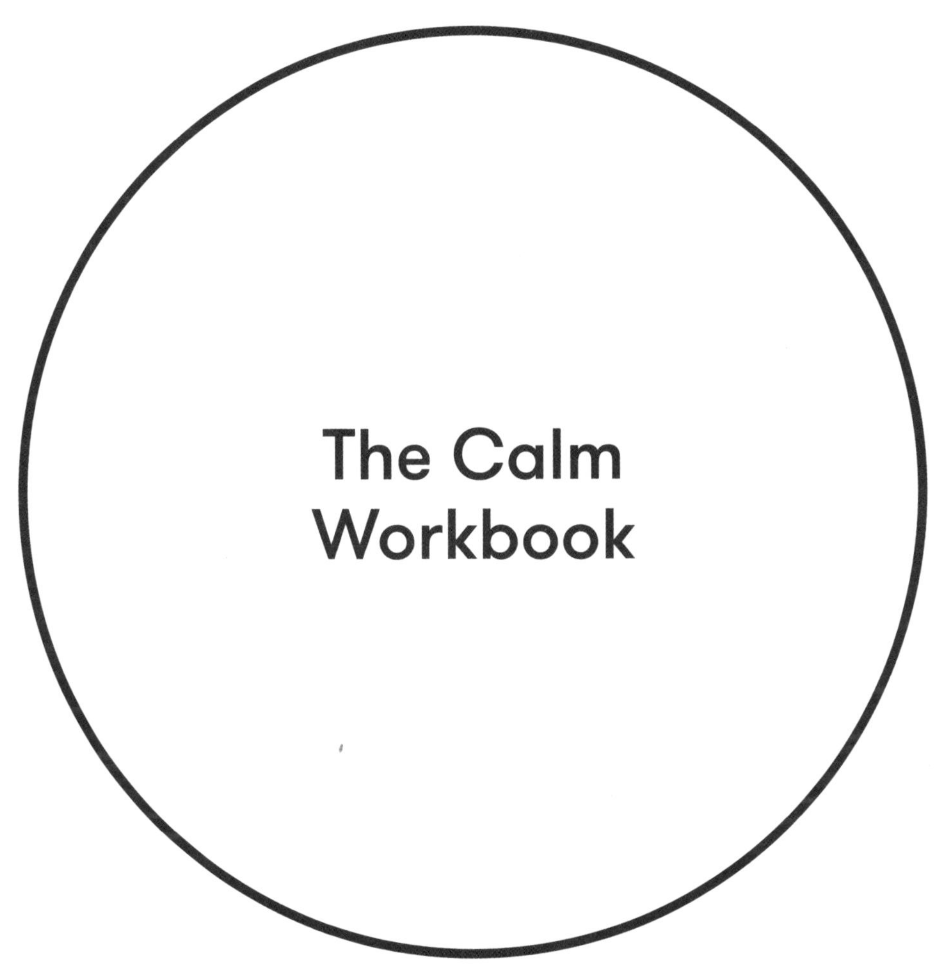

The Calm Workbook

A guide to greater serenity

Published in 2021 by The School of Life
70 Marchmont Street, London WC1N 1AB

Designed and typeset by Ryan Bartaby
Printed in China by Leo Paper

A proportion of this book has appeared online at theschooloflife.com/thebookoflife

The School of Life is a resource for helping us understand ourselves, for improving our relationships, our careers and our social lives – as well as for helping us find calm and get more out of our leisure hours. We do this through creating films, workshops, books, apps and gifts.

www.theschooloflife.com

ISBN 978-1-912891-49-8

10 9 8 7 6 5 4 3 2 1

Introduction 4

The Pledge 6

1. A Beautiful Idiot 9

2. Overcoming Anger 17

3. Melancholy Calm 25

4. The Broken Pot Exercise 35

5. Compromise 39

6. Learning to Handle Moods 45

7. Keep It Simple! 51

8. It Will Go Wrong 57

9. But You Will Survive 61

10. Global Pessimism 67

11. Sublime Views 72

12. The Catastrophe Has Already Happened 80

13. Self-Hatred and Anxiety 86

14. If You Weren't Allowed to Worry about This ... 88

15. Panic Attacks 91

16. Philosophical Meditation 94

17. Know Yourself 104

18. Living in Modernity 108

19. Telling the Story of Failure 127

20. Surrender Expectations 131

21. Impostor Syndrome 139

22. The Call of Death 143

23. Ecce Homo 145

24. You Are 'Good Enough' 147

25. Inner Voices 151

26. Remaining Calm around Other People 157

27. Care around the News 163

28. History and the News 167

29. No One Is Normal 171

30. A Quiet Life 173

31. Small Pleasures 177

32. Teasing Oneself 179

33. Keeping Faith with 'Rupture' and 'Repair' 181

34. Cheerful Despair 187

Introduction

This is a workbook about calm that recognises from the outset that attempting to be a permanently calm person is an impossible (and even dangerous) dream. There are too many reasons for us to be agitated for much of the time:

- We are intensely vulnerable physical beings: a blood clot the size of a grain of sand may kill us, an average life expectancy is only ever that and we are almost bound to be currently ignoring key bits of nutritional and medical advice.
- We have insufficient information upon which to base most of our life decisions: we steer largely blind when it comes to deciding on our careers or marriage partners, our economic choices or the welfare of those we love.
- We dwell in competitive, media-driven societies which imbue us with a sense that there is so much more we could achieve if only we were better able to understand ourselves and our opportunities. We have never done enough and, measured against what we might have been, we almost always prove a severe disappointment to ourselves.
- We are regularly panicked by news organisations which give us a picture of living on a chaotic planet fated to be destroyed and presently inhabited by billions of largely unstable and murderous fellow humans.
- Many of us have been through extremely complicated childhoods which have led us to be suspicious of ourselves, afraid of others, fearful of committing to love and sure that we deserve punishment.
- The progress of our careers and of our finances plays itself out within the tough-minded, competitive, random workings of an uncontained economic engine.
- We rely for our self-esteem and sense of comfort on the love of people we cannot control and whose needs and hopes will never align seamlessly with our own.

It is compelling to think that it would be possible to achieve permanent calm. But this hope can itself become a source of agitation. Setting our sights on an unreachable goal is destined to lead to frustration and disappointment. We should never seek the total elimination of anxiety. We should not – on top of everything else – be anxious that we are anxious. We should practise a degree of acceptance. Anxiety is no sign that our lives have gone wrong, merely that we are alive. We should spare ourselves the burden of loneliness; everyone is more anxious than they are inclined to tell us. We've collectively failed to admit to ourselves what we are truly like.

Nevertheless, we are all capable of improving a little on our capacities for calm in the face of inevitable frustrations and losses. To do this, we should graciously understand that maintaining calm is a fiendishly difficult project that requires us to submit to education. We're going to have to go back to school. Yet we can have faith that even if our lives are currently rather fraught, they are almost always open to being changed and improved – so long as we practise and build calming rituals into our days and nights.

This workbook brings together a wide range of exercises that can help us to accept ourselves more readily, soothe our worries about the uncertainties of the future, appease our rage against people who deny us our wishes and prepare us to greet life – every now and then, when we've had enough sleep – with a little more humour, benevolence and gratitude. The notion of practice is well understood in many areas – riding a bicycle or learning a new language, for example – and we should grant that it applies equally well to the field of calm. No one is intuitively good at calm. We all need to do a little homework.

Through this book, we confront a strange but important thought: that calm is a skill, not an emotion – and that we owe it to ourselves and our loved ones to undergo a few playful, intriguing and consoling exercises that can improve our capacity to maintain our poise.

Instructions on how to fill in this book

Throughout these pages, you will find sections highlighted in blue.

Take time to fill in as many exercises as feels comfortable.

Do not worry if you fall behind.

The Pledge

A calm life isn't one that's always perfectly serene. It is one where we are committed to recovering more readily after we have panicked, where we strive for more realistic expectations, where we can understand better why certain problems are occurring and where we can be more adept at finding a helpful perspective. The progress is painfully limited and imperfect – but it is genuine.

An irony is that the more calm matters to us, the more we stand to be aware of all the very many times when we have been less calm than we might have been. It can feel laughably hypocritical. Surely a genuine devotion to calm would mean ongoing serenity? But this isn't really a fair judgement to make, because being calm all the time isn't a viable option. What counts is the commitment we are making to the idea of being calmer.

We've got a mistaken picture of what the lover of calm looks like; we assume them to be among the most tranquil of the species. We're working with the highly misleading background assumption that the lover of something is the person who is really good at it. But the person who loves something is often the one who is hugely aware of how much they lack it, and therefore, of how much they need it.

For this reason, before attempting any of the exercises in this book, we want you to consider signing a declaration. We are interested in intentions, not (yet) in action.

If you can sign up to these words, however many anxieties you may have held or rages you may have fallen into, however hard serenity might appear to be, then half the battle at least has already been won.

I am deeply attracted to calm.

Collectively, calm is extremely difficult: our species is ill-suited for long periods of tranquillity.

Individually, I have been through a range of experiences which have taught me (falsely but persuasively) that anger and agitation might often be the best or only course.

Sometimes, I will be unsuccessful in my attempts to become a calmer person. That is normal. I will not let this hold me back. Instead, I will endeavour regularly to practise ideas that could make things a little more manageable.

Signed:

1.
A Beautiful Idiot

We spend a lot of time trying to avoid the idea that we might be foolish and even slightly ridiculous. We are terrified of being seen as an idiot – and tend anxiously to reassure ourselves of our dignity and seriousness. And yet, paradoxically, the more rigidly we lay claim to an always-impressive adult competence, the more our (inevitable) lapses from this state must end up agitating and shaming us. In the name of greater calm, it may be the moment to accept with courage and equanimity that we are – in fact – at many points precisely what we have always feared we might be: an idiot.

To bring this idea home, let's try to remember moments of particular idiocy in a range of areas:

Where I have been an idiot

When I've tried to flirt with someone, I …
have judged or criticized them

When trying to impress someone at work, I …
have misjudged how much they cared about it

When trying to open doors, I …
pushed instead of pulled

Sometimes food has ended up on my …
breasts

Let's consider the future. If we were to act on certain of our ambitions, how might we fail and look ridiculous?

Where I might be an idiot in the future

If I … make a bold statement as fact that is untrue

If I … thinking people support me but don't

If I …

If I …

At many moments of underconfidence, we are faced with two contrasting emotions: a *wish* and a *fear.*

We wish to seem:		We fear we are:	
Competent	*Self-contained*	*Needy*	*Eccentric*
Worldly	*Elegant*	*Naïve*	*Unfashionable*
Adult	*Composed*	*Childish*	*A mess*

The normal way that people suggest to us that we become calmer is to try to resolve the oscillation in favour of the wish. They try to reassure us that we are – despite our doubts – in reality competent, elegant, composed – and so on. What we are really not – these kindly people say – is an idiot.

This is very well-meaning and very kind, but it doesn't work. Rather than clinging to an account of ourselves as even-tempered and rational, we should make ourselves at peace with the thought that we are all – in reality – deeply and pervasively foolish. There are no other options for a human to be. We lie, we steal, we slander, we've got weird habits, we get up to funny stuff in the night, we bump into doors, we fart, we look ridiculous, we have odd thoughts and dreams … In short, we mess up.

In 1559, the Dutch artist Pieter Bruegel the Elder made a painting representing human nature. In a crowded canvas, he showed us what he thought people were actually like – which was, he sought to emphasise, completely demented.

Importantly, the painting is *not* an attack on just a few unusually mad people. It's not saying those people over there are the idiots. *It is deliberately a picture of parts of all of us.*

Strangely, this idea can prove very helpful in calming us down. There's a type of stress that arises specifically when we grow too attached to our own seriousness – and become anxious around any situation that might show up our idiocy. We hold back from challenges in which there is any risk of ending up looking ridiculous – which comprises, of course, almost all the most interesting situations.

The moral of the painting is that everyone is pretty much entirely deranged:

Here's a man throwing his money into the river.

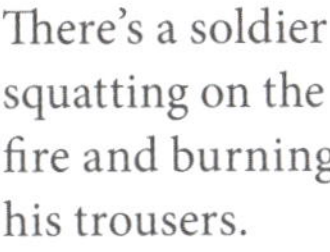

There's a soldier squatting on the fire and burning his trousers.

Someone is intently bashing his head against a brick wall.

Someone else is biting a pillar.

Pieter Bruegel the Elder, *The Dutch Proverbs*, 1559

Your own Bruegel

We're assuming you can't draw very well – almost no one can. But this isn't the point. On the canvas below, draw your own version of a Bruegel, illustrating some characteristically idiotic things you might have done or be planning to do. You might call the picture *Idiot-Me*.

In a concerted bid never to look foolish, we get anxious and miss out on the best opportunities of our lives. We imagine that it might be possible to place ourselves beyond idiocy. We trust that it is an option to lead a good life without regularly making a complete idiot of ourselves. It isn't.

We should repeat to ourselves a basic mantra:

The Idiot Mantra

I may blunder,
I may look absurd in the eyes of others,
I may say something out of turn,
I may be unwanted,
I may know no one,
I may inadvertently shock,
I may misread the situation,
And on this basis: I am human.

Once we learn to see ourselves as foolish, it really doesn't matter so much if we do one more thing that might seem quite stupid. The person we try to talk to at a party could indeed think us ridiculous. The individual we ask directions from in an unknown city might regard us with contempt. But if these people do so, it won't be news to us; they will only be confirming what we have already gracefully accepted in our hearts: that we, like them – and every other person on the Earth – are nitwits. Once we accept that failure is the norm, the fear of humiliation can no longer stalk us in the shadows of our minds. The risk of trying and failing has its sting substantially removed. We can grow free to give things a go. And every so often, amid the endless rebuffs we will have factored in from the outset, it will work: we'll get a date, we'll make a friend, we'll get a raise.

The road to greater calm begins with a ritual of telling oneself solemnly every morning, before heading out for the day, that one is a muttonhead, a cretin, a dumbbell and an imbecile. One or two more acts of folly should, thereafter, not matter very much at all.

If you could accept with good humour that you are (like all of us) a beautiful idiot, what might you dare to try next?

Once you know you're an idiot, what might you not worry about so much any longer?

To bring home the lesson about your idiocy with particular vigour, we recommend a physical exercise: *the idiot dance.*

Dancing is an activity that many of us – arguably those of us who might most need to do it – are powerfully inclined to resist and, deep down, to fear. We stand on the side of the dance floor, appalled at the possibility of being called to join in; we attempt to make our excuses the moment the music begins; we take pains that no one will ever, ever see our hips unite with a beat. *We're so worried about looking like an idiot* … We are missing the point.

The whole idea of redemptive, consoling, cathartic dancing is a chance to look like a total, thoroughgoing idiot – the bigger the better.

The idiot dance

We should put on 'Dancing Queen', 'I'm So Excited' or 'We Are Family'. We should let rip with a playlist that includes 'What a Feeling', 'Dance With Somebody' and 'I Will Survive'. We should lose command of our normal, rational selves, abandon our arms to the harmonies, throw away our belief in a 'right' way to dance or indeed to live.

There should be at least ten minutes of idiot dancing a week.

2.
Overcoming Anger

There are many negative things in our lives – but the way we respond to them is not always the same. There is a crucial distinction to observe:

A distinction in how we respond to:

Things that make us angry	*Things that make us sad*

Please fill in the following table:

What makes me angry	What makes me sad

One of the things we immediately observe is that the difference between the angry things and the sad things has nothing necessarily to do with the scale or seriousness of the issue:

- You could be *sad* that your grandmother has died, but *angry* that you can't find your pencil.
- You could be *sad* that your early promise as a violin player hasn't been fulfilled, but *angry* that your child hasn't put the top back on the orange juice.

Both anger and sadness start off with a frustration, with a wish that has not been fulfilled. But the frustration will make us *sad* when it is *expected*. And *furious* when it is a *surprise*.

Frustration + Surprise = Anger

Frustration + Expectation = Sadness

What makes us angry are frustrations, large or small, that we haven't budgeted for; that we didn't expect to happen; that we were innocent about.

Paradoxically, people who end up getting angry a lot are, in the background, operating with very high expectations. We could even say that they are, in fact, strangely optimistic.

Angry people are optimists.

They don't *seem* optimistic, of course.

When you see an angry person in a rage, they appear extremely dark. But – we insist – they are, beneath all that, still at heart optimistic. They have refused to expect frustration. They have assumed that their wishes would sail through reality unscathed.

One major way to reduce anger is more regularly to expect that bad things will happen to us. We must try to move as many of the items on the chart we just made from Column A (What makes me angry) to Column B (What makes me sad).

We need to learn the art of intelligent, pre-emptive pessimism. We must learn to expect frustration so that life doesn't surprise us at a time of its own choosing. We always have to be sad in many areas, but we don't always need to be furious.

Beneath many of the things that make us angry lies an implicitly (and recklessly) optimistic world view. We don't generally realise the absurdity of this world view until it's pointed out – so it's worth teasing it out so that we might gently correct it and therefore be less surprised by reality:

What makes me angry	I believe in a world in which …
She's half an hour late – again!	*People are always completely on time*
The pizza is cold!	*Underpaid delivery drivers always provide the best possible pizza*
There's so much traffic!	*The roads are always traffic free*
Where are the damn keys?	*Keys, and other household items, never go astray*
Stop making that chewing sound!	*Nice people have no coarse bodily habits*

Write down some of your own frustrations, along with the optimistic world view from which they must spring:

What makes me angry	I believe in a world in which ...

A pessimist is someone who assumes from the outset, and with a great deal of justification, that things tend to turn out really very badly in almost all areas of existence. Strange though it can sound, pessimism can be one of the greatest sources of human serenity and contentment.

There are so many good reasons to be a bit pessimistic: relationships are full of missed connections; sex is invariably an area of tension and longing; creative endeavour is pretty much always painful, compromised and slow;

any job – however appealing on paper – will be pretty irksome in many of its details; children will always resent their parents, no matter how well-intentioned and kindly they may be. Politics is evidently a process of muddle and uncomfortable compromise. Try filling out the following list:

What will probably go wrong in my life

In love:

Around sex:

In work:

With family:

Around health:

In politics:

This might sound like a curious and grim exercise, but we should remember that our satisfaction in this life is critically dependent on our expectations. The greater our hopes, the greater the risks of rage, bitterness, disappointment and a sense of persecution.

Like optimists, pessimists would like things to go well. But by recognising that many things can – and probably will – go wrong, the pessimist is well placed to secure the good outcome both of these parties ultimately seek. It is the pessimist who, having never expected anything to go right, tends to end up calm – and with one or two things to smile about.

In what areas of your life could you learn to be a little more pessimistic than you are now?

....

....

....

The French philosopher Nicolas Chamfort (1741–1794) arrived at possibly the best piece of advice with which to navigate through life:

'A person should swallow a toad every morning to be certain of not encountering anything more revolting in the day ahead.'

Suggested morning thought exercise*

=

Serenity

*Do not try this at home.

3.
Melancholy Calm

The goal of learning the art of pessimism isn't to be depressed – it's to know how to practise the noble art of being melancholic.

Our era isn't very interested in melancholy. Instead, it directly and indirectly tends to promote two alternative emotions in particular:

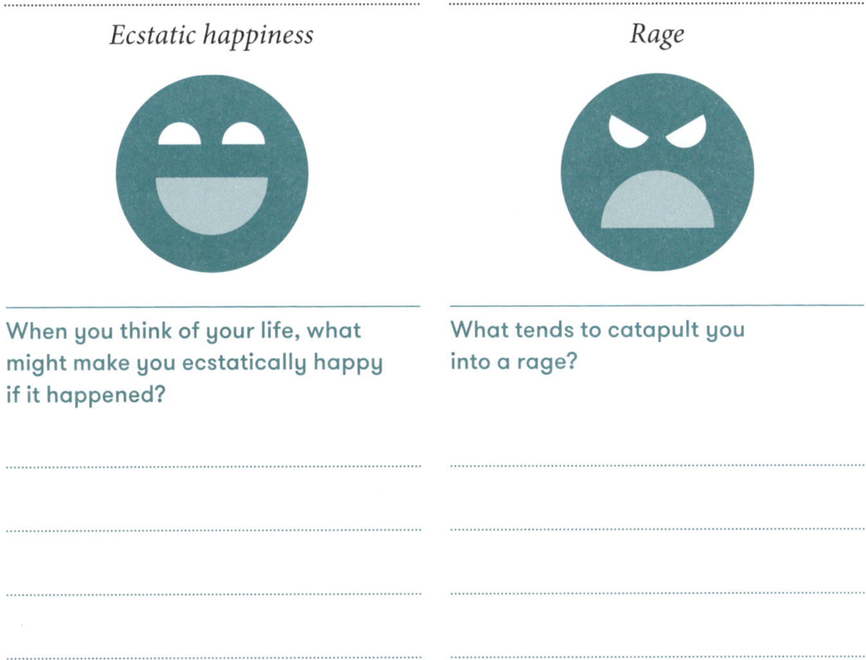

Ecstatic happiness

Rage

When you think of your life, what might make you ecstatically happy if it happened?

What tends to catapult you into a rage?

But the truth is that there is in general very little *opportunity* for ecstatic happiness and little *justification* for rage. We would be wiser to aim for the middle position of *melancholy*.

Being melancholy doesn't have to mean being grumpy. Depicted in art, melancholy faces are often not smiling but not angry either. Instead, they look lost in thought, absorbed by their own ideas and wistful rather than desperate. They know that life is often sad – it doesn't surprise them and therefore throw them into fury; they're just slowly digesting disappointment while maintaining equanimity.

(Top) Rogier van der Weyden, *The Magdalen Reading*, c. 1438;
(Bottom) Giovanni Bellini, *Madonna and the Child between Saints Catherine and Mary Magdalene [detail]*, c. 1490.

Melancholy can seem mature and intelligent.

Melancholy is not rage or bitterness; it is a valuable species of sadness that arises when we are open to the fact that life is inherently difficult for everyone and that suffering and disappointment are at the heart of human experience. It is not a disorder that needs to be cured; it is a tender-hearted, calm, dispassionate acknowledgement of how much pain we must inevitably all travel through.

Modern society tends to emphasise buoyancy and cheerfulness. It is impatient with melancholy states and wishes either to medicalise them – and therefore 'solve them' – or deny their legitimacy altogether.

Melancholy links pain with wisdom and beauty. It springs from a rightful awareness of the tragic structure of every life. We can, in melancholy states, understand, without fury or sentimentality, that no one truly understands anyone else, that loneliness is universal and that every life has its full measure of shame and sorrow. The melancholic knows that many of the things we most want are in tragic conflict: to feel secure and yet to be free. To have money and yet not to have to be beholden to others. To be in close-knit communities and yet not to be stifled by the expectations and demands of society. To travel and explore the world and yet to put down deep roots. To fulfil the demands of our appetites for food, exploration and sloth and yet to stay thin, sober, faithful and fit.

The wisdom of the melancholy attitude (as opposed to the bitter or angry one) lies in the understanding that we have not been singled out; that our suffering belongs to humanity in general. Melancholy is marked by an impersonal take on suffering. It is filled with pity for the human condition.

The more melancholy a culture can be, the less its individual members need to be persecuted by their own failures, lost illusions and regrets.

Start to think in a more melancholy way

Run through issues in your professional, personal, family and political life. Fill in the table – and try to move items over into the melancholy table.

Optimistic position:
It would be so great if …

Furious position:
This is outrageous and appalling.

Melancholy position:
It's not perfect, but that's often how things go.

Let's look at a theory that comes from a mid-20th-century psychoanalyst called Melanie Klein, who was born in Vienna and moved to London in middle age, where she was a pioneer in the psychoanalysis of children.

She is best remembered today for an unlikely-sounding but inherently sensible theory, advanced in her book *The Psychoanalysis of Children* (1932), about a 'good breast' and a 'bad breast'. We mustn't take the theory utterly literally. It's a metaphor for what it means to grow up – and to be melancholic rather than in a rage.

Melanie Klein

Klein argued that in the early weeks and months, the mother is not even a 'mother' to her child; she is – to come to the crux of the issue – just a pair of breasts that appear and disappear with unpredictable and painful randomness.

In relation to the mother, the infant experiences two things:

1. Moments of intense pleasure

When the breast is there and a feed is going well. A primordial calm and satisfaction descends upon the infant: it is suffused with feelings of well-being, gratitude and tenderness (feelings that will, in adulthood, be strongly associated with being in love – a feeling where breasts continue to play a notable role for many).

2. Moments of horrible suffering

When the breast isn't there, when the milk isn't flowing or when the mother is being frustrating in some way or other.

This difference led the baby, thought Klein, to adopt a primitive defence mechanism against what would otherwise be intolerable anxiety. The baby 'splits' the mother into two very different breasts: a 'good breast' and a 'bad breast'.

The bad breast is the target of all the disappointment and sadness and rage that the infant feels.

The good breast is the source of love, adoration and intense desire.

With time, in healthy development, says Klein, this 'split' heals. *The child gradually perceives that there is only one mother.* There is *no entirely good and no entirely bad breast*, both belong to a mother who is a perplexing mixture of the positive and the negative: a source of pleasure and frustration, joy and suffering. The child (for, by now, we are talking of someone aged around four years old) discovers a key idea in Kleinian psychoanalysis: the concept of *ambivalence*.

To be able to feel ambivalent about someone is, for Kleinians, an enormous psychological achievement and the first marker on the path to genuine maturity. For Klein, loving people and things intensely and then hating them just as intensely the moment they let you down a bit isn't passionate or romantic. It's a sign of still being very little inside.

Realising the mother is good and bad belongs to what Klein called 'Depressive Realism'.

Depressive Realism is a fancy term for being a *calm melancholy* grown-up and realising that no one and nothing can be 'perfect' – it's always a mixture of positive and negative.

Unfortunately, in Klein's analysis, not everyone makes it to the depressive position, for some get stuck in a mode of primitive splitting. For many years, even into adulthood, they must either hate or love. In relationships, they tend to fall violently in love and then – at the inevitable moment when a lover in some way disappoints them – switch abruptly and become incapable of feeling anything any more. These unfortunates are likely to move from one lover to another or one job to another, always seeking a vision of complete satisfaction, which is repeatedly violated by inevitable flaws in reality.

We don't have to believe in the literal truth of Klein's theory to see that it has value for us as an unusual but useful representation of maturity. The impulse to split people into those that delight us (give us milk, love us, keep us happy) and those that frustrate us (tell us bad news, boss us around, don't fix everything) can be painfully observed in emotional life generally. Under Klein's direction, we can see that the task is to accept life as a source of both pleasure and pain.

We are talking here about the benefits of seeing things in grey, rather than always only in black and white.

Black, white and grey

Scan through your life and fill in things that feel very 'black': people you are furious with, situations you find intolerable, things that worry you immensely.

Then scan through things that feel very pure and ideal; put these in the white section. This might be a certain lover, a job you hope for, a holiday you want to go on.

Then move the items over into the grey section, which is the perspective of melancholy. Observe what happens to them when they stop being either brilliant or appalling.

4.
The Broken Pot Exercise

The Western ideal of beauty: Sèvres porcelain, 1867

The fanciest, most prestigious Western ceramic manufacturer is probably French Sèvres porcelain. The company was financed by Louis XV and his mistress Madame de Pompadour in 1738 and turned out beautifully symmetrical, elegant, perfectly balanced tableware, which was bought by royalty and aristocracy across Europe for enormous prices. Here is an example of two lavishly painted and gilded vases from 1867.

Now look at this tea bowl, from an unknown Raku ware workshop, made in the same century as the French vases. It could be mistaken for a bit of rubbish due to its unassuming appearance, and yet it's fascinating and deeply instructive to learn that in Japanese Zen Buddhist aesthetics, this pot is viewed as a pinnacle of art worthy of immense reverence and respect.

Tea bowl, Japan, 19th century

The reason for this is that the East and the West have traditionally had two very different relationships with the idea of beauty.

The Western tradition	**The Eastern tradition**
A cult of perfection	*A cult of imperfection*

Fascinatingly, this has been reflected in ceramics. Over the centuries, Zen Buddhist philosophers developed an argument that pots, cups and bowls that had become damaged shouldn't simply be neglected or thrown away. They should continue to attract our respect and attention and be repaired with enormous care – this process symbolises a reconciliation with flaws and mistakes, reinforcing some big underlying themes of Zen.

The word given to this Zen tradition of ceramic repair is kintsugi:

Kin = golden	*Tsugi* = joinery

Kintsugi means, literally, 'to join with gold'. The broken pieces of an accidentally smashed pot should be carefully picked up, reassembled and then glued together with lacquer inflected with a very luxuriant gold powder. There should be no attempt to disguise the damage; the point is to render the fault-lines beautiful and strong. The precious veins of gold are there to emphasise that breaks have a philosophically rich merit all of their own.

Because our societies are so obsessed with perfection, the art of kintsugi retains a particular wisdom – as applicable to our own lives as it is to a broken pot. We shouldn't just focus on succeeding; we should learn the art of failing well, of handling our flaws with dignity.

This matters because we are, all of us, a bit like broken pots – and the more we accept this, the less we will rage at and feel bitter about existence.

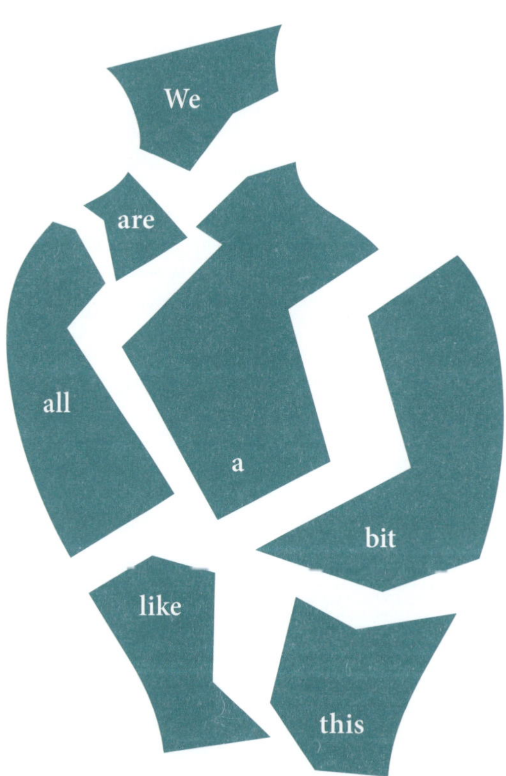

In what ways are you a smashed pot? In other words, what are your major flaws, difficulties, tragedies?

What would fixing look like? How might a 'repaired' you look? Imagine yourself mended but not invisibly repaired by any means.

5.
Compromise

We often reserve some of our deepest scorn for people who compromise: they stay in a job because they need the money; they remain in a couple for the children, or because they're scared of being lonely, or maybe they're just worried that anyone else they found wouldn't be much better.

In what areas of life would you refuse to compromise?

Compromise often seems disgraceful on account of a background belief that circulates powerfully through the collective modern psyche. This is the idea that anyone who applies their mind and will sufficiently won't have to 'make do' in any area; that there are perfect, profoundly fulfilling options available for all of us and the only things that could stand in the way of discovering them would be laziness and cowardice, flaws of character that deserve no particular sympathy or forgiveness.

Our high expectations can make us impatient around, and agitated about, those who can't attain them – which might often be us.

But imagine if we were to tweak the premise of the argument a little and for a moment probe at the notion that there really might be a pain-free option available for all of us at all times. What if our choices were, in fact, often rather more limited than modern society tends to propose? Maybe there actually aren't as many attractive, unattached people in our vicinity as there might be. Maybe we lack the charm, the personality, the confidence or the looks to attract the ones that do exist. Maybe time is running out. Maybe there aren't any perfect careers for us. Or maybe our children really would take it extremely badly if we dynamited the family for the sake of better sex and greater cheer elsewhere.

At the same time, maybe the current situation – while clearly a compromise – is not without its virtues. A partner may be only half right, often maddening and disappointing in certain areas, but – humblingly – still more satisfying than being alone. Having children to feed may make it OK to work for a company about which one has a long, only semi-private list of reservations.

The capacity to compromise is not always the weakness it is described as being. It can involve a mature, realistic admission that there may – in certain situations – simply be no ideal alternatives. And, conversely, an inability to compromise does not always have to be the courageous and visionary position it is held to be by our perfectionist ideology: it may just be a slightly rigid, proud and cruel delusion. Mocking people who compromise is – of course – emotionally very handy. It localises a problem that it's normal to want to disavow: that a degree of sadness may just be an intrinsic, unavoidable part of our lives.

Wiser societies would be careful never to stigmatise the act of compromise. It is painful enough to have to compromise; it is even more painful to have to hate oneself for having done so. We should rehabilitate and occasionally honour the ability to put up with an imperfect life, to calmly face our disappointments without falling into rage or despair, to reconcile ourselves to our damaged appearance and character and to accept that there may be no better way for us to live, given who we are and what the world can provide.

Imagine what life might be like if you better learnt to compromise in a few key areas.

If I learnt to compromise around …	I might find that …
Relationships	
Sex	
Money	
Status	
Work	
Travel	
Housing	
Politics	

High expectations are the secret cause of a great many of our agonies. We are not always humiliated by failing at things; we are only humiliated if we first invested our pride and sense of worth in a given achievement and then did not reach it. Our expectations determine what we will interpret as a triumph and what must count as a failure. 'With no attempt there can be no failure; with no failure no humiliation. So our self-esteem in this world depends entirely on what we back ourselves to be and do,' wrote the psychologist William James. 'It is determined by the ratio of our actualities to our supposed potentialities'. Thus:

$$\textit{Self-esteem} = \frac{\textit{Success}}{\textit{Expectations}}$$

The problem with the modern world is that it does not stop lending us extremely high expectations. We are constantly invited to dream. Today you may be a little short of cash, low on prestige and bruised by rejection. But these are – so it's insinuated – transient troubles. Hard work, a positive attitude and bright ideas have every chance of breaking the deadlocks in due course. It's all a question of willpower. Modernity never ceases to emphasise that success could, somehow, one day be ours. And in this way, it never ceases (gently) to torture us.

What expectations might you be prepared to dial down in the name of higher self-esteem and greater calm?

Current dangerously high expectations

Redesigned, wiser expectations

6.
Learning to Handle Moods

Far more than we are inclined to accept and sometimes even realise, we are creatures of mood: that is, our sense of our value as human beings is prone to extraordinary fluctuation. At times, we know how to tolerate ourselves, the future seems benevolent, we can bear who we are in the eyes of others and we can forgive ourselves for the desperate errors of the past.

And then, at other points, the mood dips and we lament most of what we've ever done; we see ourselves as natural targets for contempt; we feel undeserving, guilty, weak and headed for retribution and disaster.

But it can be very hard to grasp what causes our moods to shift. A day that started with energy and hope can, by lunchtime, end up mired in anxiety and pessimism. A sure sense that we've finally turned the corner and are on the way to better things can be replaced at speed by an alternative certainty that we are doomed.

We cannot, it appears, ever prevent our moods from being subject to change, but what is open to us all is to learn how to manage the change more effectively – so that our downturns can be ever so slightly more gentle, our worries more containable and our inconstancy less shameful in our own eyes.

Here is some of what we might learn to bear in mind around our seemingly unaccountable moods:

Realise our vulnerability

We should acknowledge how vulnerable our moods are to being perturbed by so-called 'small things'. We belong to a species of extreme but also fateful sensitivity; we shouldn't expect to be able to appreciate a Mozart aria or a Rembrandt self-portrait on the one hand and then, on the other, stay unbothered by the downturned corners of the mouth of a lover or the slightly distant gaze of a friend. We shouldn't berate ourselves for how thin our skin is; we should adjust ourselves to the full consequences of our extraordinary openness to experience.

Edit our social lives

Unless we take vigorous measures to edit our social lives, we can too easily find ourselves in the company of people who, though they may call themselves our friends, are – in terms of what they do to our moods – no such thing. Beneath a veneer of kindness, these people are the bearers of latent hostility, deadly competitiveness, self-absorbed hysteria or priggish moralism. To start to be a friend to ourselves means learning to take a scalpel to our address list in order to edit out all dispiriting impostors.

Have vulnerable friendships

Conversely, a great solace for a low mood is the right sort of company: people who know how to reassure us that we still belong, that sadness is to be expected and that our errors never put us beyond compassion. These consoling souls will have suffered, they will have hated themselves and they will have learnt how to laugh at the absurdity of being human. Most importantly, when we show them our low mood, they will know how gracefully to take that most essential next step of friendship: accept our flaws and display one or two of their own.

Disregard a mood

Moods are proud, imperious things. They show up and insist that they are telling us total certainties about our identities and our prospects. But we always have the option of calling their bluff, of realising that they are only a passing state of mind arrogantly pretending to be the whole of us – and that we could, with courage, politely ignore them and change the subject. We might recognise but not give way to the mood and put a bit of distance between it and our conscious selves. We might at times even do precisely what a mood commands us not to do: go and see someone rather than cede to shame; show our face rather than give way to paranoia; go out for a walk rather than fold our limbs into the foetal position.

Keep a small pilot light of kindness

While we are being rocked by a dark mood, we should strive to keep a little light on – the light of sanity and self-kindness that can tell us, even though the hurricane is insisting otherwise, that we are not appalling, that we have done nothing unforgivable and that we have a right to be. We can strive to keep ourselves plugged in to a small pilot light of kindness until a larger sun is ready to rise once more.

Historicise our moods

Our sad moods strongly imply that they are about what lies ahead of us, but very often they exist chiefly as symptoms of a difficult past: they stem from a projected memory of people around us who once told us with particular authority that we were no good, that we would fail, that we should be ashamed of ourselves and that catastrophe was around the corner. We should learn to historicise such voices and differentiate them from a trustworthy verdict on the present. Our low moods are far more about a past we still need fully to mourn than a future there is any reason to dread.

Remember: this too shall pass

Not only do difficult moods insist that they are correct, they also seek to convince us that they are permanent. But our sense of self is naturally fluid; we are condemned to rise and fall, flow and ebb. We are, as a reality and as a metaphor, largely made of water. We shouldn't allow a misplaced ideal of permanence to add to our sorrows. Though we may be unable to shift a mood, we can at least realise that it is only ever such a thing and that, in the inestimable words of the prophets, with the help of a few hours or days, it too shall pass … .

List some of your key moods and how you might now interpret them:

Mood	When I feel in this mood

What I might learn to tell myself about this mood

7.
Keep It Simple!

It is well understood by good parents that life should only ever get so exciting for a baby: after friends have come around and brought presents and made animated faces, after there has been some cake and some cuddles, after there have been a lot of bright lights and perhaps some songs too, enough is enough. The baby will start to look stern and then burst into tears and the wise parent knows that nothing is particularly wrong (though the baby may, by now, be wailing); it is just time for a nap. The brain needs to process, digest and divide up the welter of experiences that have been ingested, and so the curtains are drawn, the baby is laid down next to the soft toys and soon it is asleep and calm descends. Everyone knows that life is going to be a lot more manageable again in an hour.

Sadly, we exercise no such caution with ourselves. We schedule a week in which we will see friends every night, in which we'll do twelve meetings (three of them requiring a lot of preparation), watch three films, read fourteen newspapers, change six pairs of sheets, have five heavy meals after 8 p.m. and drink thirty coffees – and then we lament that our lives are not as calm as they might be and that we are close to mental collapse. We refuse to take seriously how much of our babyhood is left inside our adult selves – and therefore, how much care we have to take to keep things very, very simple. What registers as anxiety is typically no freakish phenomenon; it is the mind's logical enraged plea not to be continuously and exhaustingly over-stimulated.

Take a look over your diary of the past thirty days:

How many nights a week did you stay up late?

How many meetings took place each day?

How many social obligations did you have?

Might it all be too much?

Here are some of the things we may need to do to simplify our lives:

Fewer people, fewer commitments

It is theoretically a privilege to have a lot of people to see and things to do. It is also – psychologically speaking – exhausting and ultimately rather dangerous. Yet we need to recognise that what is physically possible for us to achieve in a day is not, for that matter, psychologically wise or advisable. It may well be feasible to nip over to a foreign capital or two in a day and run a company alongside managing a household, but nor should we be surprised if such routines ultimately contribute to a breakdown.

Night-time sleep

Plenty of it, of course; at least seven hours. Or if we can't manage it, we need at a minimum fully to recognise how much we are deprived, so that we won't aggravate our sorrows by searching for abstruse explanations for them. We don't necessarily have to get divorced, retrain in a completely different profession or move to a new country; we just need to get some more rest.

Daytime naps

The sophistication of any civilisation could be measured via a people's readiness to accept – whatever the inconvenience – a primary role for the siesta and the extent to which that culture can accommodate it. The siesta symbolises a mature recognition of our fleshly reality and of the limits set by our biochemical make-up on our ability to think and act well. We are not being lazy; we're acknowledging that if we are to permit the best of ourselves – our calmest, most sanguine selves – to emerge, we have to do justice to our stifled yawns.

Nutrition

It is maddening to be told this constantly and in such specific and ever-changing detail, but we do – in brief – have to eat less, and eat simpler things too. The exact details of an anxious person's diet are perhaps for others to argue about, but suffice to say that it should probably involve some nuts, slices of apple, olives, apricots and coarse bread. The body needs long periods unoccupied with any sort of physical digestion to stand a chance of tackling the peculiar fruits of its turbulent mind.

Thinking

Insomnia and anxiety are the mind's revenge for all the thoughts we refuse to have consciously in the day. To find rest, we need to carve off chunks of time where we have nothing to do other than lie in bed with a pen and paper in order to think. Every hour of living requires at least ten minutes of sifting. We need to orient ourselves in the ongoing story of our lives by (as it were) looking back over the day's narrative and writing its next few paragraphs. We might conduct a Philosophical Meditation (see Chapter 16.) or a little anticipatory thinking about the challenges of the day ahead. Experiences lose at least half of their power to unnerve us when we have gone through them in our minds the day before.

Expectations

Of course, it might be pleasant to be extraordinary, famous and world-beating, but maybe it will be an even greater achievement to stay sane and kind. We are not backing away from a challenge; we're simply shifting our sense of what the real challenge might be – and more importantly, where the real rewards may lie. We might choose not to conquer the world in favour of living a longer, and more serene life. A quiet life isn't necessarily one of resignation or flight; it may constitute a supremely wise recognition that excitement is fun for a time, but it also kills. Simplicity is true wisdom; we need more naps.

How might you retool your life in the above areas? Make some pledges to yourself in the following areas:

Fewer people, fewer commitments

Nighttime sleep

Daytime naps

Nutrition

Thinking

Expectations

8.
It Will Go Wrong

The Stoic philosophers of Ancient Greece and Rome invented the term, 'premeditation' to describe a process, normally to be performed once a day in bed before getting up, whereby one looks into one's future and systematically imagines everything that could go wrong. It is a deliberate, artful, ritualised meditation on varied options for upcoming disasters.

The practice is based on the view that our minds do us an enormous disservice through their sentimental, unexamined optimism, leaving us unprepared for the catastrophes that will inevitably come our way. A premeditation constitutes a deliberate attempt to bring our expectations in line with the troubles we might face.

The Roman philosopher Seneca – possibly the greatest of all the Stoics – believed that the greatest service we can pay ourselves is to anticipate disaster. Here is one of Seneca's premeditations as an example:

> *The wise will start each day with the thought: fortune gives us nothing which we can really own. Whatever has been built up over years is scattered and dispersed in a single day. No, he who has said 'a day' has granted too long; an hour, an instant, suffices for the overthrow of empires. Look at your wrists, a falling tile could cut them. Look at your feet, a paving stone could render you unable to walk again. We live in the middle of things which have all been destined to be damaged and to die. Mortal have you been born, to mortals have you given birth. Reckon on everything, expect everything.*

Premeditation doesn't, of course, remove the bad things. But by getting us to admit, frankly and bravely, that we are likely to encounter setbacks in our lives, it can leave us a little less distraught when they eventually come our way.

Design your own premeditation

1. What are you hoping for?

Premeditate that it won't happen.

2. Who do you rely on?

Premeditate that they will let you down.

3. Who do you love?

Premeditate that they will leave you.

4. What are you proudest of?

Premeditate that it will be ruined.

5. Do you love your reputation?

Premeditate on its destruction.

6. Do you expect to live long?

Premeditate on your possible death before tonight.

7. Does the ground seem solid?

Premeditate on an earthquake.

Seneca tells us that we must grow familiar with, and hold before us at all times, not just the sort of events we like to plan for, that are recorded in living memory or are common in our age group and class, but the entire range of possibilities – a longer and inevitably far less agreeable list which finds space for cataclysmic fires, sackings and deaths. It is the unexpected that catches us out.

> *Nothing ought to be unexpected by us. Our minds should be sent forward in advance to meet all problems, and we should consider not what is wont to happen, but what can happen.*

At one point, a friend of Seneca's named Marcia was devastated by the death of her son, Metilius, not yet twenty-five. She fell into a period of mourning that seemed to have no end: three years after the death, her sorrow had not abated; indeed, it was growing stronger every day. To lose a son was surely the greatest grief that could befall a mother, but given the vulnerability of the human frame, Metilius's early death was not outside the merciless natural order, which daily offered examples of its handiwork. So Seneca sent her an essay in which he expressed the hope that, given the length of time that had elapsed since Metilius's death, she would forgive him for going beyond the usual condolences to deliver something darker, but perhaps more effective. He wrote:

> *We never anticipate evils before they actually arrive, but, imagining that we ourselves are exempt and are travelling a less exposed path, we refuse to be taught by the mishaps of others that such are the lot of all. So many funerals pass our doors, yet we never dwell on death. So many deaths are untimely, yet we make plans for our own infants: how they will don the toga, serve in the army, and succeed to their father's property.*

They might fulfil all these plans, but how mad to love them without remembering that no one offered us a guarantee that they would grow to maturity, let alone make it to dinner time.

> *No promise has been given you for this night – no, I have suggested too long a respite – no promise has been given even for this hour.*

If Metilius's death had been unexpected for Marcia, it was only on the basis of a wishful assessment of probabilities.

> *You say: 'I did not think it would happen.' Do you think there is anything that will not happen, when you know that it is possible to happen, when you see that it has already happened to many?'*

What do you imagine won't ever happen to you – though it does happen to a lot of other people?

....

....

....

....

....

....

Now – for your sake, for the sake of calm – imagine that it might …

9.
But You Will Survive

A lot of agitation boils down to a single fear:

If X happens,	*I won't be able to survive ...*
(Part A)	*(Part B)*

Notice that there are two parts to that statement, A and B. Most of the time, when people are trying to calm us down, they focus on addressing part A. They spend their time telling us that what we fear will happen, won't happen. This is meant very kindly and it works in the short term, but it doesn't properly help and, in the long run, does us a serious disservice.

At The School of Life, we recommend a different route concerning part B: we suggest that you look squarely at what you think you won't survive and realise that, in one way or another, you will. It might be pretty tough, and 'surviving' might be a long way from thriving, but you will get through it one way or another. Increasing our own sense of resilience is vital to calming ourselves down.

It is possible to work on our impression of our survivability. We are, in fact, far stronger than we think; a lot of what we have right now, we could lose and do without. We may believe that we'd be broken by various sorts of frustrations and losses, but we could withstand them. We could lose:

- our health
- our partner
- our job
- our status

And it would be, not pleasant, but survivable.

The way to convince ourselves of this is to think through in detail how life would be possible in a reduced state. We mustn't leave our fears at the back of our minds, unexamined and toxic. We need to bring them out in broad daylight and submit them to reason. We need to envisage a survivable reduced existence.

Don't Think	Think
I won't lose the money	*I could be OK with less*
The new business venture will succeed	*I'll be alright even if it goes belly up*
My relationship will improve	*It'll be bearable even if it never does*

Resilient Thinking is the opposite of Optimistic Thinking. Optimistic Thinking focuses on the sunny upside scenario. Resilient Thinking focuses on the very grimmest scenario and investigates in detail how it would be endurable.

Let's look at how Resilient Thinking works:

Terrible Fear	Resilient Thinking
I might get sacked	Huge drop in income Nine months' unemployment Tension at home Two years' retraining *Survive!*
My partner might leave me	Six months of agony Hysterical crying every night Unable to contemplate ever seeing anyone again Greatest betrayal ever One day, under pressure from friends, another date Almost back to normal after three years *Survive!*
I might get a serious illness	Twelve months of horrendous drugs Lose hair Lesions on skin Feel sick all the time Lose job Be looked after at home Three years' rehabilitation *Survive!*

I might get a very serious illness	Three weeks left to live Quick goodbyes to everyone Die *'What other end is there for a human being?'* – Marcus Aurelius

To return to the Stoics: a lot of Seneca's thought is known to us from the letters he wrote to his friends, giving them counsel in times of trouble. Seneca, had a friend called Lucilius, a civil servant working in Sicily. One day, Lucilius learnt of a lawsuit against him which threatened to end his career and disgrace his good name. He wrote to Seneca in a panic.

'You may expect that I will advise you to picture a happy outcome, and to rest in the allurements of hope,' replied the philosopher, but 'I am going to conduct you to peace of mind through another route' – which culminated in the advice: 'If you wish to put off all worry, assume that what you fear may happen is certainly going to happen.'

This is an essential Stoic tenet. We must always try to picture (or *premeditate*) the worst that could happen – and then remind ourselves that the worst is survivable. The goal is not to imagine that bad things don't unfold; it's to see that we are far more capable of enduring them than we currently think.

To calm Lucilius down, Seneca advised him to make himself entirely at home with the idea of humiliation, poverty and ongoing unemployment – but to learn to see that these were, from the right perspective, not the end of everything.

'If you lose this case, can anything more severe happen to you than being sent into exile or led to prison?' asked the philosopher, who had himself survived bankruptcy and eight years of exile in Corsica. 'Hope for that which is utterly just and prepare yourself for that which is utterly unjust.'

Seneca gave Lucilius a meditation to mull over in the luxury of his home that he was now in danger of losing: 'I may become a poor man; I shall then be one among many. I may be exiled; I shall then regard myself as born in the place to which I shall be sent. They may put me in chains. What then? Am I free from bonds now? Behold this clogging burden of a body, to which nature has fettered me!'

Following Seneca's example, we should practise Resilient Thinking scenarios. We should imagine how we'd survive if we lost our money, our reputation, our friends, our health … Instead of letting fears creep up on us, we should dare them to do their worst and see that we could endure them: disgrace, poverty, disease … They aren't desirable, of course, but they can be mastered, and this is what we should put a high degree of mental effort into right now, when things might still be more or less OK. We should move from dimly being terrorised by spectres to asking ourselves directly and on a regular basis how we might cope.

Resilient disaster planning

In the space provided, prepare answers to the following disasters:

Catastrophe	How I could cope
Being sacked	
Being disgraced	
Being abandoned	
Falling seriously ill	
Falling into poverty	

10.
Global Pessimism

We are recommending pessimism. However, we can distinguish between two kinds of pessimism:

- Local Pessimism
- Global Pessimism

Local Pessimism involves getting sad about one particular area of frustration and no more. It is for those moments when the car ahead of us stalls just as the lights turn; when our partner is 26-minutes late (already), though they promised that this time they'd be punctual; when we're just settling down in a café to do some work and realise we've forgotten to charge the laptop; when there's a particularly wrong-headed article in the newspaper … It is modest in intent, but its tone can appear peevish, mean-spirited, provincial and a little bitter.

Global Pessimism sees that, in a curious – and important – way, our ire is misdirected. We're maddened by a specific detail when the real cause of our frustration is, in reality, much grander and more general. It is in essence the human condition – the metaphysics of life – that distresses us so much and with which we are constantly colliding in small ways and large.

Global Pessimism makes no reference to any catalyst for gloom, and simply makes large statements about humanity and its doomed nature. It can appear, in contrast, Olympian, calm, world-weary and even darkly funny.

We are suggesting that it is infinitely better to say:

'All human conversation is pointless.'
(Global Pessimism)

Than to remark:

'Mum is so stupid in how she doesn't listen.'
(Local Pessimism)

Local Frustration	Local Pessimism	Global Pessimism
My child spilled rice all over the floor	*My child isn't neat*	*Children are a lifelong punishment for a few moments of sentimentality*
My flight has a four-hour delay	*Flights get delayed*	*All of man's unhappiness comes from the inability to stay alone in his room*
They've turned me down for sex	*Sex is frustrating*	*No one understands anyone*

Philosophy provides us with some truly delightful examples of Global Pessimism. For example, the 19th-century German philosopher Arthur Schopenhauer.

Here are some of his great sayings:

'It may be said of life: it is bad today and every day it will get worse, until the worst of all happens.'

'Every life history is a history of suffering.'

'The only people we can think of as normal are those we don't know very well.'

'The best cure for love: to get to know them better.'

'After his fortieth year, any man of merit will hardly be free from a certain touch of misanthropy.'

'Human life must be some kind of mistake'

It should be no surprise to us that the calmest person who ever lived, Buddha, carried with him only one super-generalised statement of Global Pessimism, which served him hugely well in a wide variety of settings:

'Life is suffering.'

Equally prescient was our friend Seneca, who wrote:

'What need is there to weep over parts of life? The whole of it calls for tears.'

Reading the mordant pronouncements of Global Pessimism could be depressing, but it isn't.

Firstly, if we're not ourselves sad, we can derive a new sense of how lucky and favoured we are.

Secondly, if we are sad, we no longer feel so alone. Moreover, the exaggerated tone makes us feel that someone else might even be slightly sadder than we are, which is always a little uplifting. Global Pessimism does naturally involve exaggeration – but an exaggeration of the darkness that serves us very well.

Turn some of your local frustrations into globally pessimistic pronouncements:

Local Frustration	Local Pessimism	Global Pessimism

Here is Seneca in a 19th-century painting, shown just after having committed suicide by slitting his wrists – having been ordered to do so by his former pupil, the demented Roman Emperor Nero.

Manuel Domínguez Sánchez, *The Death of Seneca*, 1871

11.
Sublime Views

Sometimes we respond quite negatively to encounters with things that are much larger and more powerful than ourselves. It's a feeling that can strike us when we are alone in a new city, trying to negotiate a vast railway terminal or the huge underground system at rush hour, and we sense that no one knows anything about us or cares in the least for our confusions. The scale of the place forces upon us the unwelcome fact that we don't matter very much in the greater scheme of things, and that the things that are of great concern to us don't figure much at all in the minds of others. It's a potentially crushing, lonely experience that intensifies anxiety and agitation.

But there's another way an encounter with the large scale can affect us – and calm us down.

Artists and philosophers have given this feeling a name: the Sublime. We experience this sensation of the Sublime whenever we are hugely impressed by something that seems much larger and more powerful than we are. It might be the beauty of a verdant valley, a majestic view of the mountains, or the vastness of the ocean that overwhelms us with its grandeur while also offering us a vivid sense of our own relative insignificance. At this moment, nature seems to be sending us a humbling message: the incidents of our lives are not terribly important in the scheme of things. And yet, strangely, rather than being distressing this sensation can be immensely comforting and calming.

The Sublime is calming because it counteracts a persistent and very normal source of distress in our lives. Our minds naturally focus on what is immediately before us. We instinctively get deeply engaged with whatever happens to be close to us in space and time. And we have a proportionally less intense, more detached relationship to things that feel very far off. It's not a surprising arrangement. Very often what's immediately present is more relevant to our survival than what happened five years ago or might happen much later in our lives. Our minds are geared towards fleeing a snake or staving off hunger. Translated into the terms of modern life, it means that last night's squabble over flecks of toothpaste on the bathroom mirror and the work deadline of Tuesday morning feel hugely agitating – even if, in terms of the overall meaning of a relationship, a career or a whole life, they are in fact pretty minor incidents. The problem is, our minds are structured so as to give maximum attention to what is happening now, whereas to see the true importance of anything, we have to situate it in a much larger frame of reference. In the bigger picture, the squabble and the deadline really might not be so crucial.

What the Sublime does is – very unusually – foreground our engagement with the larger horizons of existence. Instead of looking at this or that detail (which therefore seem very big, because they dominate the current moment) we've got an experience in which the specific details of our lives are seen as proportionally much smaller and therefore as posing a far less significant threat to us. Things that have, up to now, been looming large in our minds (what's gone wrong with the Singapore office; the fact that a colleague behaved coldly; the disagreement about patio furniture) tend to get cut down in size. The Sublime drags us away from the minor details which normally – and inevitably – occupy our attention and makes us concentrate on what is truly major. Local, immediate irritants are reduced, for a while, in their power to bother us.

At present, our beneficial meetings with the Sublime occur pretty much at random. One just happens to see an amazing sunset or chances to look out of the window of the plane when it's passing over the Dolomites or the Taurus Mountains. But this doesn't tie in with an understanding of its place in our emotional lives – if we see what it can do with us, we shouldn't leave that to chance; we should be strategic about it and 'make appointments' with deserts, glaciers and oceans on a regular basis.

We've got a model for how to do this. Religions have often ensured that their followers would regularly meet with the Sublime in a cathedral or church somewhere not very far from where they lived. They constructed buildings specifically designed to awe the congregation and they didn't just hope that people would drop by. They put a date in the diary, every week.

Similarly, we might structure our encounters with the Sublime through works of art.

Meditations on sublime works of art

Spend one minute (that can feel surprisingly long) looking at the images on the following pages.

Caspar David Friedrich, *Reefs by the Seashore*, 1824

A striking, jagged rock formation, a spare stretch of coast, the bright horizon, far away clouds and a pale sky … We might imagine walking along this coastline in the predawn, after a sleepless night, on the bleak headland, away from human company, alone with the basic forces of nature. The smaller islands of rock, each swept endlessly by the grey sea, were once as dramatic and thrusting as the major formation just beyond. The long, slow passage of time will, one day, wear them down as well. The first portion of the sky is formless and empty, a pure silvery nothingness, but above that are clouds which catch the light on their undersides and pass on in their pointless, transient way, indifferent to all of our concerns.

This picture does not refer directly to our relationships or to the stresses and tribulations of our day-to-day lives. Instead, it gives us access to a state of mind in which we are acutely conscious of the largeness of time and space. The work is sombre rather than sad; calm, but not despairing. And in that condition of mind – that state of the soul, to put it more romantically – we are left, as so often with works of art, better equipped to deal with the intense, intractable and particular griefs that lie before us. The tensions in your relationships or the frustrations of your work are not your problems alone they are part of the structure of the universe …

What do you see?

Large Magellanic Cloud, NGC 1872, 2010

Somewhere here, though the untrained eye does not know where to look, a star is in the final stages of a cataclysmic explosion. The unimaginably vast residue of its matter, which was pulled together so infinitesimally slowly and which burnt for aeons in a blinding furnace of power, is finally flung back into the universe. Science joins art to dignify and lend tragic grandeur to our inescapable fragility. We do not know what will happen in our lives; where we will end up; what will befall those we love; what will be the results of our efforts; whether our devotions will bear fruit; whether our hopes will be fulfilled or whether our dreams realised or dashed. This image can guide us to a helpful perspective. It offers to soothe our worries about next week by holding our attention to something vast and impersonal. We are reminded of how minor our preoccupations can look. The problem isn't that we worry about next week – rather we tend to fret unproductively; to dwell on worries without resolving them. The image helps break that circuit. We will, of course, have to face next week when it comes. But we can do so a little refreshed, thanks to a few moments with a globular cluster.

How do you feel?

Hiroshi Sugimoto, *North Atlantic Ocean, Cliffs of Moher*, 1989

There is no very definite horizon in the photograph, just a gentle zone of transition where the sea merges with the sky. The black at the bottom becomes the white at the top through a multitude of tiny stages. This has a tranquillising effect which has a chance to enter into our being and adjust how we respond to challenges and anxiety.

A tranquil state of mind is supremely valuable in connection with many of the lesser troubles of life. At times, we should know how to close down our hopes and give ourselves over to the contemplation of all that we will never be able to alter, here symbolised by the even, pure tones of an eternal horizon.

To those of us in need of calm, this photograph might capture an attitude of mind to be summed up in times of trial.

Let your eyes wander over the vast grey swell of the sea and immerse yourself in the attitude of serene indifference it invites. Write down any thoughts that come to mind.

12. The Catastrophe Has Already Happened

Anxiety belongs in every life. But in some lives we can fairly say that it has become so constant that it has become unnecessarily punishing. What can explain persistent, high-level anxiety that goes beyond – far beyond – ordinary worry?

We might venture that somewhere in the history of the constantly worried, the bit of our mental equipment designed to distinguish between modest and extreme danger has taken a hit. The very worried have – somewhere along the line – received such a very big fright that pretty much everything has now grown frightening. Every slightly daunting challenge becomes a harbinger of the end; there are no more gradations. The party where one knows no one, the speech to delegates, the tricky conversation at work … these put the whole of existence into question. Pretty much every day is a crisis.

Let's go in for a metaphor. Imagine that, at a formative moment, when the very anxious would have been profoundly unprepared and without the resources to cope, they had an encounter with a bear. The bear was beyond terrifying. It raged, it stamped, it crushed. It threatened to destroy everything: it was incomprehensibly, mind-defyingly awful. As a result, the anxious person's inner alarm jammed into the 'on' position and has stayed stuck there ever since. There is no use casually telling this person that there aren't any bears around at the moment, or that this isn't bear season, or that most bears are kind, or that campers rarely encounter them. That's easy for you to say – you who have never woken up with a giant grizzly staring at you with incisors showing and giant paws held open for the kill.

The result of this bear encounter is an unconscious commitment to catastrophic generalisation; the very anxious fear all bears, but also all dogs, rabbits, mice and squirrels, and all campsites and all sunny days, and even associated things, like trees rustling in the wind, or prairie grass, or the smell of coffee that was being made shortly before the bear showed up. The very anxious can't do logical distinctions; they can't rank threats accurately.

To start to dig ourselves out of the quicksand of worry, we – the very anxious – need to do something that is likely to feel artificial and probably rather patronising too. We need to learn – on occasion – to distrust our senses completely. These senses, which are mostly terrific guides to life, have to be seen for what they also are: profoundly unreliable instruments, capable of throwing out faulty readings and destroying our lives. We need to erect a firm distinction between feelings and reality; to grasp that an impression is not a prognosis, and a fear is not a fact.

One side of the mind has to treat the other with a robust, kindly scepticism: 'I know you're sure there is a bear out there (at that party, in that newspaper article, in that office meeting). But is there one really? *Really* really?' Emotion will be screaming 'Yes!' like one's life depends on it. But we've been here before and we need – with infinite forbearance – to let the screaming go on a little – and ignore it entirely. The cure lies in watching the panic unfold and in refusing to get involved in its seeming certainties.

To get better, which really means to stop dreading bears everywhere, we need to spend more time thinking about the specific bear that we once saw. The impulse is to focus always on the fear of the future. Instead, with compassion and in kindly company, we need to direct our minds back to the past and revisit certain damaging scenes. A consequence of not knowing the details of what once scared us is a fear of everything into the endless future. Now we should ask: What sort of bear was it? What did it do to us? How did we feel? We need to relocalise and repatriate the bear, to get to know it as a spectre that happened at one point, in one place, so that it can stop haunting us everywhere, for all time.

That we were once very scared is our historical tragedy; the challenge henceforth is to stop giving ourselves ever newer reasons to damage the rest of our lives with fear.

Where was the bear?

The leading symptom of trauma is to be tortured daily by a feeling of imminent catastrophe. Something terrible seems about to happen to us. That fear leads to a state of hypervigilance, where we are permanently on the alert, permanently worried, permanently scared and permanently really very unhappy.

People may try to reassure us, but reassurance goes nowhere; the terror remains.

One way to break the deadlock is to try to go back to the catastrophe that has been forgotten and that is making us sick with worry. If the future is to get brighter, we will need to remember the catastrophe and locate it where it really belongs: safely, but also poignantly and tragically, in the past.

Think of a recent moment when you have felt gripped with anxiety. What was the trigger? Looking back, can you think of a time when you felt that feeling as a child? Now look at that moment and notice the specific details. Who was there? What was the weather like? What were you wearing? If you felt at fault, was it actually your fault or was anyone else taking part? Remember, you were just a child.

Psychological trauma can be defined as a negative event so overwhelming that one cannot properly understand, process or move on from it, but – and this is the devilish aspect to it – nor can we easily remember it or reflect upon its nature and its effects on us. It may be lodged within us but remain hidden from us, making its presence known only via symptoms and pains, altering our sense of reality without alerting us to its subterranean operations. Traumatised people don't go around thinking that they are unnaturally scared; they just think that everything is terrifying. They don't notice their appallingly low sense of self-worth; they just assume that others are likely to mock and dislike them.

Predictably, a lot of psychological trauma happens in childhood. Children are especially vulnerable to being traumatised because they are not yet able to understand themselves or the world very well – and have to rely almost exclusively on parents who are frequently less than mature, patient or balanced. A child may, for example, be traumatised by a parent who – through no particular fault of their own – becomes heavily depressed shortly after childbirth. Or a child may be traumatised through exposure to a parent's titanic rage or violence. Or because the widest category of psychological trauma is also the most innocuous, a child may be traumatised by what psychologists term 'neglect', which might mean that, at a critical age (between 0 and 5, and especially in the first 18 months), it was not properly cherished, soothed, comforted and – to use a large but valuable word – loved.

The legacy of having been traumatised is dread – an unnameable, forgotten, unconscious memory of terror and fear projected outwards into the future. As the psychoanalyst Donald Winnicott observed: 'The catastrophe one fears *will* happen has *already* happened.' That is why, to find out the gist of what might have happened to us long ago, we should ask ourselves not so much about the past (we won't directly be able to remember), *but about what are we afraid will happen to us going forward.* Our apprehension holds the best clues to our history.

Uncovering and overcoming trauma is the work of years – and in deep-seated cases often requires the help of a wise and clear-eyed friend or therapist – but the beginning of the end starts with a very small step: coming to realise that we might actually be traumatised and that the world may not be the dark, overwhelming and dread-filled place we had always assumed it had to be.

Uncovering the source of trauma

It is strange that we should have forgotten the catastrophe. But that's the point with trauma: it disappears from memory. It is too painful to be held in active consciousness, to be processed and verbalised – and it therefore gets pushed into the unnameable, unknown zones of the mind, where it creates ongoing havoc.

To start to master trauma, we can reverse-engineer a picture of what must have happened long ago, in years that we can't now easily think about; we can take what we fear of the future and picture that a version of this terror actually already unfolded. The best clue as to the nature of our difficult past lies in our fears of the future.

What I fear will happen in the future	What happened in the past
I'm going to be abandoned	
I'm going to be shamed and humiliated	
I'm going to be publicly mocked	

I'm going to lose physical control over myself	
I'm going to be seen as a loser, weirdo or monster	

The logic of the exercise dictates that we should, for every entry on the left, be able eventually to think of an entry on the right. But bringing this to the surface is liable to be immensely difficult. We can't do it on command. It requires time, very relaxed circumstances, perhaps music, a long train or plane journey, a chat with a friend or therapist, a night or two when we stay up very late with a pen and paper and no phone and just think while the rest of the world sleeps.

But eventually, some memories are likely to resurface, along with a lot of sadness and (ideally) compassion for ourselves. We aren't about to be revealed as monsters; we have – already – been made to feel like monsters. We aren't about to be abandoned; we have already been left …

This doesn't mean that there is never anything to be afraid of in the present. But we have to distinguish between abject terror and fear. There are things to fear in the here and now, but these aren't things to be terrified of – and for one central reason: because we are adults and it is the privilege of adults to have basic freedom, agency and independence. We could take action, were bad things to happen to us, in a way that children who were traumatised never could. Life may yet get very tricky for us, but we never need be as terrified of it as we were when the original catastrophe occurred. With sufficient exploration of the past, the terror of what is ahead could – just – be relocated to the category of historic trauma, where it truly belongs.

13.
Self-Hatred and Anxiety

The temptation, when dealing with anxiety, is always and invariably to focus on the ostensible cause of our worry: the journey to the airport, the forthcoming speech, the letter one is waiting for, the presentation one has to hand in …

But if we proceed more psychologically, we might begin in a different place. With great kindness and no disrespect, we may step past the objective content of anxiety and look instead at something else: how the anxious person feels about themselves.

An unexpected cause of anxiety is self-hatred. People who have grown up not to like themselves very much at all have an above-average risk of suffering from extremes of anxiety, for if one doesn't think one is worthy, it must – by a dastardly logic – follow that the world is permanently and imminently at high risk of punishing one in the way one suspects one deserves. It seems to fit that people may be laughing behind one's back, that one may soon be sacked or disgraced, that one is an appropriate target for bullying and rejection and that persecution and worse may be heading towards one. If things seem to be going well, this must just be the deceptively quiet period before others realise their error and mete out some horrific punishment. For the self-hating, anxiety is pre-emptive anticipation of the pain one unconsciously feels one is owed; very bad things must and should happen to very bad people.

Part of the problem and one of the curious aspects of the way our minds work is that it isn't always clear that one is even suffering from low self-esteem; hating oneself has just become second nature rather than an issue one has the will to rebel against or even so much as notice. To tease out the sorrow and start to feel it again (as a prelude to treating it), one might need to fire a few questions at oneself.

A self-esteem questionnaire

1. Broadly speaking, I like myself as I am.	◯ Agree strongly ◯ Agree ◯ Neither agree nor disagree ◯ Disagree ◯ Disagree strongly
2. People should be relatively grateful to have me in their lives.	◯ Agree strongly ◯ Agree ◯ Neither agree nor disagree ◯ Disagree ◯ Disagree strongly
3. If I didn't know myself, I'd think I was OK.	◯ Agree strongly ◯ Agree ◯ Neither agree nor disagree ◯ Disagree ◯ Disagree strongly
4. Growing up, I was given the feeling that I properly deserved to exist.	◯ Agree strongly ◯ Agree ◯ Neither agree nor disagree ◯ Disagree ◯ Disagree strongly

If one finds oneself at the disagreeing end of such questions, it may be that one is an agitated person not because one has more to worry about, but because one likes oneself rather less than normal – and certainly less than one fairly should.

The cure isn't, therefore, to try to dispel anxieties with logic; it is to try to dispel it with love; it is to remind the anxious person (who may be ourselves) that we are not inherently wretched, that we have a right to exist, that past neglect wasn't deserved, that we should feel tenderly towards ourselves – and that we need, both metaphorically and probably practically too, a very long hug.

The logic of this analysis is truly counter-intuitive. It suggests that when panic next descends, one should not spend too long on the surface causes of the worry, but instead try to address the self-hatred fuelling the agitation. Anxiety is not always anxiety; sometimes it is just a very well-disguised, entrenched and unfair habit of disliking who we are.

14.
If You Weren't Allowed to Worry about This …

One of the most difficult features of anxiety is that it tends to be all-consuming. It squats in the middle of our minds and refuses to let anything else in or through. Our thoughts become low, relentless, repetitive, stymied things, returning again and again to the issue of whether the door is locked, the accounts were signed off or the social media account is not under attack. Anxiety dominates and excludes any other form of mental activity; all that will be in our minds is terror. Impregnable and bullying, anxiety in effect shuts down our central faculties.

But there is one nimble way to try to outwit anxiety – and that is with a question that recognises a fundamental feature of anxiety: that it is frequently a smokescreen for something else, something beyond what we consciously think is worrying us, that we're in fact concerned with or sad about.

One of the peculiar facets of our minds is that we may choose to feel anxious rather than to confront things that may be yet more painful or emotionally awkward in our lives. It can be easier to fret than to know ourselves properly.

We might feel anxious about whether we're going to get to the airport on time as an escape from the greater challenge of wondering whether this holiday is even worth it and whether our spouse still loves us. Or we might get intensely anxious about a financial issue in order to avoid a yet trickier acknowledgement of our confusion at the course of our emotional lives. Or we may develop a sexual anxiety as an alternative to thinking about our sense of self-worth and the childhood that destroyed it. Panic may be invited to shield us from more profound sources of self-aware agony.

And yet, of course, we are always better off getting to the root cause of our troubles, rather than filling our minds with diversionary panic – and in order to do so, we would be wise at points to ask ourselves a simple but possibly highly revealing question:

'If your mind wasn't currently filled with these particular anxious thoughts, what might you have to think about right now?'

The question, as simple in structure as it is acute in design, is liable to unlock a moment of original insight.

The answer might go like this:

- I might realise how sad and lonely I am …
- I might realise how angry I feel towards my partner …
- I might realise how abandoned I feel …

And that, of course, is precisely what we should be doing now: processing all the stuff that our anxiety was trying to keep at bay.

Certain anxieties can be taken at face value, for they do clearly relate to worrying things in the world. But there is another class, and a rather large one at that, that is there for no better purpose than to distract us from understanding important parts of ourselves. If we need to suffer, and often we will, the least we can do is to ensure that we are suffering for the right reasons.

At points, we should trade our anxiety in for something far more important: a confrontation with the real ambivalence and complexity of our lives – and we should do so thanks to a naïvely simple question:

'If your mind wasn't currently filled with these particular anxious thoughts, what might you have to think about right now?'

15.
Panic Attacks

During a panic attack, the pervasive worry that we normally carry within us and that is typically content merely gently to corrode away our lives promptly changes tack and decides it might try to kill us off instead – preferably very soon.

We're meant to give an hour-long speech in a couple of minutes, but we stand petrified in the wings of the theatre, our mouth entirely dry, our heart racing and our mind unable to remember so much as the first letters of the alphabet, let alone what our name is.

The aeroplane doors close and we realise that we won't be able to get off for six hours, that we can hardly move our legs without touching passengers on every side, that the air we're breathing has passed through the lungs of 200 other people (and a couple of jet engines too) and that we're going to be a few miles off the ground – and the whole situation suddenly seems wholly surreal, tear-jerkingly cruel and deeply unsurvivable.

Or we're at a business meeting, surrounded by colleagues and prospective clients, and we're made aware that our bowels are about to open or our stomachs to heave their contents across the table and that we'll be publicly reduced to a pure emanation of noxious sludge – after which it would evidently be best not to try to continue with one's life and instead to be taken away, done in and never mentioned again.

What are we to do at such moments? What could the most well-wrought philosophy do for us when we're about to soil ourselves or start wailing uncontrollably at the back of a tightly packed Airbus?

There might, despite everything, be a few shreds of advice to hold on to:

First, we should embrace the situation. Though this seems like the oddest and most embarrassing thing ever to have unfolded, it happens all the time, even to good, decent people who are worthy of respect and will enjoy a lengthy and dignified old age. This is not the end, though – of course – it feels exactly like it.

Secondly, accept the fear; don't fight it. It's like trying to wrestle with the current – best to let the waves carry one this way and that; they'll tire eventually and set one back on shore. Never struggle against a riptide. Accept that maybe the speech won't happen; you might faint in your seat or be forced to run out of the room. So what? Refuse to be humiliated by the panic. You don't have to be competent all the time. Everyone is allowed some failures and this just happens to be one of your well-earned ones. You are not made of glass.

Thirdly, at the height of the fear, it can help to get deeply but redemptively pessimistic about everything. Though it seems like everything matters intensely, gloriously, in truth, nothing matters at all. Almost every human on the planet is entirely indifferent to you. Out in the Mojave Desert, scorpions are scuttling among the rocks; an eagle is soaring above the Karakoram Pass; up there in the universe, the two moons of Mars, Phobos and Deimos, are completing their orbits. You will soon enough be dead, properly inert rather than merely scared, and it will have been as if you never existed. You are but a blip in eternal cosmic time; whether your speech unfolds well or badly, or you soil your trousers or not, is a matter of sublime, beautiful indifference to planet Kepler-22b, 600 light-years from Earth in the constellation of Cygnus.

Fourthly, when calm has returned, try to think all this through, ideally with a kindly friend or therapist. It's to do – perhaps in part – with a baseline sense of unworthiness. You don't, at some level, feel it's permissible for you to give a speech and impress a hundred people or succeed in your career. Maybe, in your unconscious, this might make someone (a parent?) feel jealous or inadequate – and it's kinder, therefore, to stick to being small and unobtrusive.

To which the answer is to reassert, in the light of day, the basic truth that you have every right to exist and draw pleasure from this life; that there is nothing illegal about having a positive effect on others; that you can be a decent colleague, friend, parent and citizen – and make it to the bathroom on time. You are allowed to be.

Also, consider that the panic might have to do with a memory of long ago having been controlled, hurt and not allowed to get away. It's an aeroplane door that has just closed, but in the unconscious mind, it's perhaps also symbolic of a return to other situations of powerlessness that were unmasterable and that continue to haunt you.

To which the answer is to go back to the past, understand it fully and drain it of its power to upset the present. The memories need to be heard and the trauma digested. Meanwhile, the plane is going to take off and the doors will eventually open again, and one will be free to go wherever one wants because one is now an adult, with all the agency and liberty that word should imply.

Or maybe what powers your terror is a feeling that you have to impress other people and won't be forgiven if you don't. To which the answer is that you're OK just as you are; the days of having to impress are over; you need to prove nothing at all. There is no need to let self-contempt keep tearing you apart.

Lastly, don't avoid everything that scares you; don't let the panic reduce you. Don't accord the fear so much respect that you start to listen to its tyrannical dictates.

Answer the aggression within every panic attack with its opposite: a deeply unconditional love towards yourself, its unfortunate, blameless, worthy and loveable victim.

16. Philosophical Meditation

A lot of the reason why we lose our calm is that we have not given ourselves the proper time to think.

We hear a lot – nowadays – about the practice of meditation. In standard meditation, we strive to empty consciousness of its normal medley of anxieties, hurts and excitements and concentrate on the sensations of the immediate moment, allowing even events as apparently minor but as fundamental as the act of breathing to be noticed. In a bid for serenity and liberation, we still the agitations of what Buddhists evocatively term our 'monkey minds'.

But there is another approach to consider, based not on Eastern thought, but on ideas transmitted to us via the Western tradition. In Philosophical Meditation, instead of being prompted to sidestep our worries and ambitions, we are directed to set aside time to untangle, examine and confront them.

It is a distinctive quirk of our minds that few of the emotions we carry in them are properly acknowledged, understood or truly felt; that most of our affective content exists in an unprocessed form within us. Philosophical Meditation seeks to lend us a structure within which to sieve the confused content that muddies our stream of consciousness.

Key to the practice is regularly to turn over three large questions:

What am I anxious about?

We are rarely without a sizeable backlog of worries, far greater than we tend consciously to recognise. Life, properly felt, is an infinitely alarming process even in its calmer stretches. We face a medley of ongoing uncertainty and threats. Even ordinary days contain concealed charges of fear and challenge: navigating through a train station, attending a meeting, being introduced to a new colleague, being handed responsibility for a task or a person, keeping control over our bodies in public settings – all contain grounds for agitation that we are under pressure to think should not be taken seriously.

During our meditative sessions, we need to give every so-called small anxiety a chance to be heard. What lends our worries their force is not so much that we have them, but that we don't allow ourselves the time to know, interpret and contextualise them adequately. Only by being listened to in generous, almost pedantic detail will anxieties lose their hold on us. At almost any time, a chaotic procession flows without our minds that would make little sense if recorded and transcribed: '… biscuits to the train why earrings deal they can't do it I have to Milo phone list do it the bathroom now I can't do, 11:20, thirty-three percent it a 10:30 tomorrow with Luke why invoices separately detailed why me trees branches sleep right temples …'

But such streams can gradually be tamed, drained, ordered and evaporated into something far less daunting and illogical. Each word can be encouraged to grow into a paragraph or a page and thereby lose its hold on us. We can force ourselves to imagine what might happen if our vague catastrophic forebodings actually came to pass. We can refuse to let our concerns covertly nag at us and look at them squarely until we are no longer cowed. We can turn a jumble of worries into that most calming and intellectually noble of documents: a list.

What am I upset about?

This may sound oddly presumptuous, because we frequently have no particular sense of having been upset by anything. Our self-image leans towards the well-defended. But almost certainly, we are somewhere being too brave for our own good. We are almost invariably carrying around with us pulses of regret, loss, envy, vulnerability and sorrow. These may not register in immediate consciousness, not because they don't exist, but because we have grown overly used to no one around us giving a damn and have taken heed, along the course of our development, to recommendations that we toughen up.

Yet a life among others daily exposes us to small darts and pinpricks: a meeting ends abruptly; a call doesn't come; an anticipated reunion feels disappointingly distant; someone doesn't touch us when we needed reassurance; news of a friend's latest project leaves us envious. We are mental athletes at shrugging such things off, but there is a cost to our forbearance. From small humiliations and slights, large blocks of resentment eventually form that render us unable to love or trust. What we call depression is sadness and anger that have for too long not been paid their dues.

During a Philosophical Meditation, we can throw off our customary and reckless bravery – and let our sadness take its natural, due shape. There may not be an immediate solution to many of our sorrows, but it helps immeasurably to know their contours. As we turn over our griefs, large and small, we might imagine we were entertaining them with an extremely kind and patient figure, who gave us the chance to evoke hurt in detail; someone with whom there would be no pressure to rush, be grown-up or impressive and who would allow us to admit without fear to the many things that have pained and reduced us in the previous hours.

What am I ambitious and excited about?

A part of our mind is forever forward-thinking and hopeful, seeking to maximise opportunities and develop potential. Much of this energy registers as vague tension about new directions we might take. We could experience this inchoate restlessness when we read an article, hear of a colleague's plans or glimpse an idea about next year flit across our mental landscape as we lie in the bath or walk around a park. The excitement points indistinctly to better, more fulfilled versions of ourselves. We should allow our minds to wonder at greater length than usual about what the excitement (it could be a view, a book, a place, an insight) might want to tell us about ourselves.

In a poem written in 1908, the German poet Rainer Maria Rilke described coming across an ancient statue of the Greek god Apollo. It had had its arms knocked off at the shoulders but still manifested the intelligence and dignity of the culture that had produced it. Rilke felt an unclear excitement. He meditated upon and investigated his response, and concluded that the statue was sending him a message, which he announced in the final dramatic line of 'Torso of an Archaic Apollo':

Du musst dein Leben ändern
You must change your life

Influenced by German Romanticism, Rilke realised that he had fallen under the spell of an abstruse way of thinking and expressing himself. Now the Greek statue was being recognised by one part of his mind as a symbol of the intellectual clarity of Ancient Greece, which his conscience knew he needed to pay more attention to. By decoding his excitement, Rilke was catching sight of an alternative way of being.

The case may be particular, but the underlying principle is universal. We each face calls, triggered by chance encounters with people, objects or ideas, to change our lives. Something within us knows better than our day-to-day consciousness the direction we may need to go in to become who we really could be.

A period of Philosophical Meditation does not so much dissolve problems as create an occasion when the mind can order and understand itself. Fears, resentments and hopes become easier to name; we grow less scared of the contents of our own minds – and less resentful, calmer and clearer about our direction. We start, in faltering steps, to know ourselves slightly better.

Instructions for a Philosophical Meditation

1. Anxiety

Write down what you are anxious about; find at least eight things.

Each entry should be only a single word (or just a few words) at this point.

Don't worry if some of the anxieties look either trivial or dauntingly large. The mind tends to be an almost comedic blend of the two.

If you're having trouble, search for things that may be anxiety-inducing under the following categories:

- Work
- Relationships
- Children/parents
- Health
- Money
- Things I have to do

Feel the curious release that can come from just making a list of these items. Huge relief can come from what we call 'unpacking' an anxiety. There are two kinds of unpacking we might do around any given anxiety.

There is practical unpacking: talk yourself through the practical challenge. Ask the following questions:

- What steps do you need to take?
- What do others need to do?
- What needs to happen when?

It is very useful to have a calm and sympathetic part of yourself listening in on the detailed description of what needs to be done to address an issue. It's no longer merely an anxiety; it's a set of steps. They might not all be easy, but at least you are clearer about what they are.

There is also emotional unpacking: talk yourself through an emotional challenge or set of doubts.

Describe the feeling in more detail. What do you feel it points to? Imagine trying to piece it together for a considerate friend.

The aim here isn't to solve all anxieties; it's to get to know them and to experience the relief that comes from clarity.

2. Upset

As quickly as you can and without bothering how petty, unreasonable or pretentious it might sound, write a list of current upsets – the more the better. How have others hurt you? What are you sad, distressed, nostalgic or wounded about?

In the present safety of this exercise, allow yourself to be, for instance, furious about the way your partner brushes their teeth (too lackadaisical or too smug); the agents of global politics; your boss saying 'Yeah, right' in a slightly sarcastic manner; the hotel receptionist who implied you might not be a suitable customer; your mother commenting on your new haircut. These are just starting points; every starting point is valid.

Look at your list. Select two ways that people have hurt you that particularly preoccupy you, without considering the objective merits of your irritation. What is it about these things that bothers you? Go into as much detail as possible. Imagine you are pouring your heart out to a sympathetic and patient friend.

Now ask yourself: if this had happened to a friend, how would you advise them? What might you say?

Again, we're not attempting to resolve these issues as yet. The crucial issue is to get clear about what is actually distressing us. We're moving from vagueness to clarity.

3. Excitement

Your list might (but doesn't need to) include:

- Moments of envy: when you thought that someone else had something you might like to have a version of yourself.
- Daydreams: ideas about how life might ideally be, that you'd maybe feel awkward about telling others, because they might seem far-fetched, greedy or odd.
- How nice someone or something was.
- How thrilled someone makes you feel.

Select two items that have particularly been on your mind. Pass them through a sieve of further questions:

- Describe your excitement as if to a sympathetic, interested friend.
- If you could realistically change your life in certain ways, what would it be to change your life in the light of this?
- This exciting thing holds a clue to what is missing in your life; what might be missing?
- If this thing could talk, what might it tell you?
- If this thing could try to change your life, what changes might it advise?
- If other parts of your life were more like this, what might they be like?

It would help if we could perform a Philosophical Meditation at least twice a week.

17.
Know Yourself

Though we spend an inordinate amount of time with ourselves, strangely, it's remarkably hard to develop a proper understanding of how we operate: what we want, how we feel and why we react as we do. This lack of self-knowledge can be acutely dangerous. It makes us get into the wrong relationships, pick unsatisfactory jobs and spend money unwisely. It may also, above anything else, destroy calm. No wonder Socrates summed up all the counsel of philosophy in just two words: 'know yourself'. When we have time, we might put a number of questions to ourselves, so that we can better come to know our own interiors:

How was childhood difficult for you?
Almost everything we are today is the result of patterns laid down in childhood that we have forgotten. Children are not constitutionally made to understand their own psychology. They can tell you about distant planets way before they have any grasp of their motives or emotions. The first ten years were blind. We now have to go back and re-interpret them.

At heart, men are really ... / women are really ...
A favourite technique of psychologists is the unfinished sentence which invites us to complete it without thinking too much – so that we engage our unconscious minds and discover some important attitudes that we normally repress. Knowing yourself involves being very unfrightened about stuff. We're all extremely strange, and that's fine.

Draw your nuclear family

Include your family members, a house, a sun and a tree. This is suggestive, not science, but we have some clues about the meaning of what you've drawn below*:

*Clues as to what you've drawn:

- Who you drew yourself next to is who you are closest to.
- Who you drew furthest away is emotionally most distant.
- The size you have drawn yourself is the size of your self-esteem.
- The house is an extension of yourself: Is it in good shape? Optimistic? Ordered?
- Windows imply your degree of communication: Does your house have a door?

In love, what is your type?

The people we tend to go for may be attractive to us not only for some very nice reasons (they're friendly, are into politics or love sports), but also because they bring with them some special kind of trouble or difficulty to which we are especially prone. Most of us are involved in the compulsion to repeat certain sorts of suffering in our personal lives, normally based on the sufferings of childhood.

If someone likes me a lot, I might start to feel ...

One answer you might give is that you might start to feel a bit nauseous – and try to persecute or run away from the enthusiastic party (why do they have such bad taste?). This is a characteristic response if you have issues with liking yourself – which around half of us do (largely because important people in our past weren't that keen). Start to master your suspicion of yourself, so as not to hold it rabidly against others when they are keen.

If I knew I couldn't fail in my professional life, I'd try to ...

We are often so scared of being humiliated by the gap between our aspirations and our reality that we don't even dare to voice any aspiration – thereby conclusively ensuring that it can never come true. We owe it to ourselves to state what we, deep down, feel we could do and be – even if it never comes right.

If a really kind person wanted to praise me, they'd say ...
If a really tough person assessed me, they'd say ...

Learn to steer a good course between the two. Be the tough, generous friend to yourself.

What am I addicted to?

We operate with some stock images of the addict: a person with a heroin needle in a park, or who nurses a bottle of gin in a paper bag at nine in the morning, or who sneaks off at every opportunity to smoke some marijuana.

However dramatic and tragic such cases of addiction might be, they are simultaneously hugely reassuring to most of us because they locate the addict far from ordinary experience, somewhere off-stage, in the land of semi-criminality and outright breakdown.

The School of Life defines addiction in another way: as the manic reliance on something, anything, to keep our darker or more unsettling thoughts and feelings at bay. What properly indicates addiction is not *what* someone is addicted to, for we can get addicted to pretty much anything. It is the motives behind a reliance on a certain element – and, in particular, our attachment to it as a way of avoiding encounters with the contents of our own minds and hearts.

Facing up to ourselves is, for most of us, very understandably, a deeply anxiety-inducing prospect. We are filled with thoughts we don't want properly to entertain and feelings we are desperate not to feel. There is an infinite amount we are angry and sad about that it would take an uncommon degree of courage to face. We experience a host of fantasies and desires that we have a huge incentive to disavow, because of the extent to which they violate our self-image and our more normative commitments.

We shouldn't pride ourselves because we aren't injecting something into our veins. Almost certainly, we are doing something else to take us away from ourselves. We are checking the news at four-minute intervals to keep the news from ourselves at bay. We're doing sport, exhausting our bodies in the hope of not having to hear from our minds. We're using work to get away from the true internal work we're shirking.

To overcome addiction, we need to lose our fear of our minds. We need a collective sense of safety around confronting loss, humiliation, sexual desire and sadness. On the other side of addiction is philosophy – understood as the patient, unfrightened, compassionate examination of the contents of our minds.

18.
Living in Modernity

Personal troubles sometimes have big, historical causes

In our own lives, we typically see problems close up. There are lots of details that are getting us down: there's too much to do; we fly off the handle over little things; we worry about affording a house; our partner is too demanding; we're not sleeping very well. We might wonder what it is all for, but there isn't much time to wonder these days. We feel guilty about not getting proper exercise. We encounter the symptoms, but it's hard for us to see if there's a powerful causal factor that lies behind these localised frustrations and annoyances.

We understand this distinction between symptoms and causes in medical situations: someone might have a pain in their big toe and dry skin. The natural instinct is to think, *There's something very wrong with my toe*, because that's where the pain is occurring. But the problem isn't caused there. There's something wrong with the kidneys leading to a build-up of urate crystals in the toe joint.

In the 1960s, feminism took off by making this same move: finding a big, underlying factor that explained a lot of personal gripes and annoyances. In the late 1950s, women across the USA might have thought things like: *My husband is a bit selfish; I wish I could have an interesting job and make decent money myself; I was a fool, I should have worked harder at college, but I didn't see the point at the time; I'm not even sure I want children – does that mean there's something wrong with me?* In 1963, Betty Friedan argued that all of these complaints – which could seem like merely individual personal grievances – were in fact symptoms of a bigger issue which up to that point people hadn't identified: it was, in her words, 'the problem that has no name'.

> *The problem lay buried, unspoken, for many years in the minds of American women. It was a strange stirring, a sense of dissatisfaction, a yearning [that is, a longing] that women suffered in the middle of the 20th century in the United States. Each suburban housewife struggled with it alone. As she made the beds, shopped for groceries ... she was afraid to ask even of herself the silent question — 'Is this all?'*

Friedan reframed the issue: what's going on isn't just a local difficulty with your life. It's not something specific about your particular relationship or your career options. You are suffering from a big, historical problem. She was pointing out that women were feeling the effects of living in a society that had evolved to focus on male authority and opportunity. Women were being given access to a really big story about the origins of their sufferings (big and small).

We believe that much of our lack of calm should also be attributed to a large historical cause. In this case, the problem lies with *modernity.*

Make a list of the major issues that threaten your peace of mind.

Which feel like they are narrowly your fault and responsibility – and which feel like they could be the fault of 'history'?

'Modernity'

Modernity is the name of a phenomenon that captivated artists and writers from the middle of the 19th century. Starting in Paris and spreading to Vienna, London and New York, architects, poets, painters and novelists started responding to the vast expansion of cities, the arrival of the railways, the huge increase in newspapers and the amount of advertising that was going on all around them. But, in its more ambitious forms, modernity didn't just reflect a new subject matter. Avant-garde artists started developing new styles – they changed the *way* they painted. They went from producing highly esteemed traditional works, like those of Claude Lorrain which emphasised harmony and balance, to making things like Georges Braque's 1913 work *Nature Morte (Fruit Dish, Ace of Clubs).*

Claude Lorrain, *Landscape with Hagar and the Angel*, 1646

Georges Braque, *Nature Morte (Fruit Dish, Ace of Clubs)*, 1913

Braque and his colleague Picasso were in the process of inventing Cubism. Cubist works struck early viewers as hard to understand, as too busy and broken up. But Braque and Picasso weren't setting out to annoy people. They were signalling that something very important was happening, that life was getting more agitated, more fragmented, more sharp-edged. They started making images that reflected just these qualities.

Similar changes were taking place at the same time in literature. Traditional narrative was leisurely and clear. A very successful traditional novelist like Anthony Trollope would take care to let the reader know about what was happening. Reading a Trollope novel would be a calm, comfortable experience – maybe very slightly tedious, but definitely reassuring, as seen here in an extract from *The Prime Minister.*

Mr Wharton was and had for a great many years been a barrister practising in the Equity Courts,—or rather in one Equity Court, for throughout a life's work now extending to nearly fifty years, he had hardly ever gone out of the single Vice-Chancellor's Court which was much better known by Mr Wharton's name than by that of the less eminent judge who now sat there. His had been a very peculiar, a very toilsome, but yet probably a very satisfactory life. He had begun his practice early and had worked in a stuff gown till he was nearly sixty. At that time he had amassed a large fortune, mainly from his profession, but partly also by the careful use of his own small patrimony and by his wife's money. Men knew that he was rich, but no one knew the extent of his wealth.

Literary modernity rejected this approach. In chapter seven of his novel *Ulysses* – first published as a whole in 1922 – James Joyce describes one of the main characters, Leopold Bloom, walking into a Dublin newspaper office:

He pushed in the glass swingdoor and entered, stepping over strewn packing paper. Through a lane of clanking drums he made his way. WITH UNFEIGNED REGRET IT IS WE ANNOUNCE THE DISSOLUTION OF A MOST RESPECTED DUBLIN BURGESS ... Thumping. Thump. This morning the remains of the late Mr Patrick Dignam. Machines. Smash a man to atoms if they got him caught. Rule the world today. ... HOW A GREAT DAILY ORGAN IS TURNED OUT ... It's the ads and side features sell a weekly, not the stale news in the official gazette. Queen Anne is dead. Published by authority in the year one thousand and. Demesne situate in the townland of Rosenallis, barony of Tinnahinch. To all whom it may concern schedule pursuant to statute showing return of number of mules and jennets exported from Ballina. Nature notes. Cartoons. Phil Blake's weekly Pat and Bull story. Uncle Toby's page for tiny tots.

Understandably, sceptical readers at first simply thought that Joyce was hopeless at telling a story. It's hard to follow what's going on; it seems to be a jumble of stray thoughts. In fact, he had a serious purpose: he was trying to reproduce what he saw as the chaos of modern experience. What's going on inside our heads has become – he says – more like this: agitated, distracted, confusing.

We tend to consider modernity as an artistic, cultural movement. We need to rediscover it as something that reflects the most troubling aspects of our inner lives in the contemporary world.

Artists like Joyce and Braque are tracking a development that's still going on in our own lives: the loss of serenity. There are three deep causes of this loss of serenity: busyness, competition and envy.

In what ways can you identify your life as unfolding in a recognisably 'modern' setting?

Which of your problems can be attributed to features of modernity?

Busyness

Today, we're expected to be always busy. Take, for example, work: the idea of having precisely defined hours no longer feels normal or natural. Essentially, you are still at work if work can reach you. If you can't get out of range, you can't ever really be free. Busyness depends upon how easy it is to get a claim on your attention and make a demand. Busyness has been increasing for centuries because of developments in the technology of access.

In early 18th-century Scotland, you might turn up in midsummer at someone's house – hoping to get them to do some work for you – only to be informed that they had 'gone to London' and that they would be 'back by Christmas'. But if there was anything urgent that needed doing, you could always travel ten days and nights in a coach in pursuit of them. Or you could send a letter: it would take 110 hours and cost two shillings – two days' average wages. But soon things got faster and cheaper. Technology got more sophisticated. By 1840, a letter would only take 33 hours and cost a penny (about five pounds today). However, if your quarry had gone overseas, they would be out of reach for weeks or months. At least until 1866, when the first successful telegraph cable was laid across the Atlantic – though if they went to Australia, they were safe until 1872. From the 1930s onwards, the telex meant that work could follow you. Extensive documents and files could follow you around the globe, so you would never have the excuse of not having the relevant material to hand. But the telex system was expensive and required special operators, so there were restrictions on its use. By 1993, email solved those problems, reducing the cost of communication to almost zero – though you could very reasonably say that you didn't get the email because you were on a train, at the airport or because you had stepped out of the office to have lunch. Until 2007, that is, when the smartphone became mainstream. There are now few moments when one is legitimately beyond reach: in the shower, perhaps – though there are very good waterproof cases.

The history of communications can be told as a success story, of course. But it is also the record of the gradual and grotesque conquest of privacy. We used to be protected by impediments. People simply couldn't make demands on us – no matter how much they might have wanted to. We're not used to thinking of what the upside of impediments used to be.

At how many points in your life are you now properly 'out of contact'?

How many people on average try to contact you every day?

What effect might busyness be having on your sanity?

Competition

Competition is a key feature of the modern world, especially when it comes to our economies. Competition has been fostered by governments around the world because of the benefits it typically brings to customers and consumers: lower prices and a wider range of products. Competition is designed to benefit the customer, rather than the company. And the reward is that when we go to buy things, we are offered lower prices and a wider range of options.

The cost comes in our working lives. Greater competition makes companies fight to win sales. Customers should be very fickle. They should have a lot of choice and be very willing to go with the better deal, wherever it comes from.

Companies have to strive to lower their prices or offer better, more enticing products. A firm that stands still will be overtaken by a more innovative or more efficient rival. Competition – ideally – keeps profits in check. If a firm has a bumper year and makes a big profit, that should send a clear invitation to rival firms to move in, undercut, reduce the margins. A so-called efficient market really means one where it becomes ever more challenging to make a profit.

Internal competition in companies makes employees compete against one another. The successful may be well rewarded, but there's a permanent cull of the less efficient. And competition should also mean that many companies fail. A really efficient marketplace should be a really stressful place to work – because you're always afraid of going out of business.

We have bought our happiness as consumers at the price of ourselves as producers. We had the option of running the economy for the sake of the worker or the consumer. The idea of ourselves as consumers dominated the image of ourselves as workers. The huge collateral cost is that everyone at work is stressed. Efficiency brings anxiety, punishing hours and insecurity into the workplace. Familiar things tend to feel natural. But actually it's very odd that people in executive jobs are working so hard.

History reminds us how much beyond the normal level we are operating. The philosopher John Stuart Mill worked in London for a vastly powerful business – the East India Company – from 1823 to 1858. He was mainly involved in policy formation and finished his career in one of the most senior roles: his job title was 'The Examiner'. It was a position with a great deal of responsibility; Mill was often required to give evidence on behalf of the company before parliamentary committees. And he was very well paid. The job carried a salary of £2,000 – more than twenty times the average income. But while employed by the East India Company, Mill also managed to write some major and highly influential philosophical works – including, among many others, two monumental works: *A System of Logic* (1843) and *The Principles of Political Economy* (1848).

Mill was able to do all this because, most afternoons, the East India Company's offices were quiet. He could sit at his desk and get on with his own projects. Nobody was angry with him for doing so. If anything, they were impressed by his work ethic.

In his report for the UK government's 1864 School Enquiry Commission, the poet and civil servant Matthew Arnold advised the adoption in England of the workload for teachers in France: 'A teacher at a French Lycée has his three, four or five hours a day in lessons and conferences, then he is free.' He was specifically arguing against the practice in England of schoolteachers working a few hours a week on top of this, supervising games.

John Stuart Mill, c. 1870

Arnold and Mill – who were immensely respectable figures – show us that it was completely normal in the professional world of the mid-19th century to work around twenty hours a week. These were not people who were lazy or marginal in their careers. They used their free time in very constructive and ambitious ways. That's why it was possible for the leading philosopher to be in business and for one of the major poets to work as a senior administrative officer.

In some ways, we are simply unlucky to be living at this moment of intense commercial competition. In general, the idea of historical bad luck makes a lot of sense: people's lives just happen to get played out against the background of huge events. 1938 was an unfortunate time to turn 21.

We understand that certain times were hard. The challenge today isn't so concentrated and dramatic. But when we notice the difference between the life of Mill and our lives, it is extraordinary (that's before we even mention housing and what the average salary would have bought in London then and now). Mill and Arnold were able to hold down very good, high-level jobs for many years, but they faced nothing like the pressure and anxiety we have to live with. It's not just that a particular company is very demanding or that our own shortcomings lead to weariness and insecurity; it's the larger dynamics of market capitalism. Competition is why lunch usually means two minutes for a sandwich at the desk.

Matthew Arnold, *Vanity Fair*, 1871

Famous for taking it easy, writing poetry – and reforming the education system.

How many hours a week do you work?

Are you more prosperous or more free?

Are you content with the choice made for you by history?

Envy

In the Middle Ages, if you lived in Bristol (which was then a busy but small seaport), you probably wouldn't have known much about what was happening in London, Paris or the royal courts of Spain. Less urgent information might simply never circulate around the country: that the ladies at court like to gather their hair up in net bags on either side of their face; that they like red gauntlets sewn with pearls in floral patterns.

Blanche of Lancaster, first wife of John of Gaunt and mother of Henry IV, was the best-dressed woman in mid-14th-century England. But she couldn't be *fashionable*, because it took too long for people to find out about what she was wearing. The daughter of a well-to-do merchant in Bristol might take a great deal of interest in clothes, but she couldn't compare herself with the grander ladies of London – like Blanche – because she simply didn't know what they were up to. And in any case, Blanche hardly seemed to belong to the same species. Then, in August 1770, the first edition of *The Lady's Magazine* appeared. Every month it carried detailed illustrations of what the most prestigious women were wearing, so news about bonnets and high waists could circulate rapidly.

'London Fashionable Walking Dresses',
July 1812, published in *The Lady's Magazine*

Anyone reading this magazine could, at last, compare their own clothes with those of the rich and well connected in London, and so they were provided with the opportunity of experiencing a novel emotion: the feeling of being left out by history, by fashion, by everyone. Up until then you could be left out, of course – but only by people who you knew, who lived around you. Your cousins didn't take you berry-picking; the vicar didn't ask you to dinner. The magazine, however, presented itself as revealing what every lady in the land was wearing – except you. Actually, 'the lady' was not the disembodied voice of the spirit of the age speaking with universal authority; it was mainly concocted by a man called John Coote in a dusty little office, in an unprepossessing corner of London. The new media of the 18th century was also teaching men the pains of missing out and being left behind: a yeoman farmer could learn from *The Spectator* that he was a clodhopper; *Tatler* encouraged a local squire to recognise himself as a dull provincial. The growth of modern technology created the opportunity for comparison. It needed better roads, more efficient printing, the use of special-coloured inks, an effective postal service to get a copy of *The Lady's Magazine* into the hands of people in Newcastle and Exeter. And comparison opened the way to envy and disappointment. The 18th century was introducing the world to the distinctive modern experience of comparison.

Officially, we are simply finding out about the world; we are informing ourselves about the lives of others – their style and achievements. But we evolved as social creatures living in large groups; we're primed by nature to be very interested in social hierarchies. It seems innocuous: an article about the chicest ski resort in Europe; a photo shoot of a young woman with amazingly beautiful legs; the new trend for rooftop lap pools; a profile of how a tech titan made his billions – it's just information about what's happening around the world, but what it's doing in our heads is very harmful. Envy is dependent on knowledge and hope. We only envy things that feel as if they're within our reach. Yet the world of the magazine is highly selective. In the magazine, everyone is fashionable, everyone seems to have plenty of money, everyone is aged between 18 and 25 and has a perfectly shaped nose. Our natural instinct for comparison goes haywire as a result. By the standards of the magazine world, we are barely acceptable, we are on the lowest rung. We come away with a nagging sense of being plain, dowdy and short of cash. The life we lead – which used to seem fine – now looks so disappointing, because it compares so unfavourably with the picture of existence conjured up in the media. And so we are required to continually fight an internal battle to stave off the envy and humiliation provoked by over exposure to the lives of the freakishly successful and beautiful few.

Which celebrities make you jealous?

What publications make you feel inadequate?

In what ways do you feel that you are a lesser human being than you 'should' be?

History dignifies our problems

Looking at three big factors in modernity – the rise of busyness, the growth of competition and the vast increase in the circulation of envy-inducing information – shows that our problems are not always the result of personal failings. This doesn't make the problem go away. What it does is transform its meaning. History helps us reframe what we're going through. It guides the re-interpretation of our own experience. You understand your problem in non-hysterical, non-panicky ways. There are three specific consolations of history:

1. It depersonalises

However intimate it all feels – the exhaustion, the relationship tension, the build-up of demands, the ever-increasing expectations – the fact is that one is not alone. Because these troubles arise out of big, historical factors, they are necessarily going to be very widespread. You belong to a community of people who have this problem.

2. It shifts the direction of blame

History teaches us not to shout at the wrong person. It's not your fault, and it's not just some stupid managerial issue that's getting you down. We can grasp why the problem won't go away quickly or easily – why just changing jobs or getting divorced won't necessarily solve the issue. History offers an insight into potentially mitigating factors around work.

3. Participation in the grandeur of history

The real root of your problem is not the chaos at the office; it's this high-cultural issue known as modernity. In general, we understand how much it can mean to people to see themselves in grand historical terms. Mourners at the funeral of Winston Churchill – which took place in January 1965 – knew they were recognising more than the death of a single individual. They were collectively witnessing the passing of an epoch.

Sir Winston Churchill's funeral
procession, Fleet Street, London, 1965

The grandeur of history isn't only about positive things which are shared. There is grandeur in recognising the scale of the collective traumas we go through together – they are so much bigger than us; they set the stage on which we lead our lives; we have no control over them.

We haven't yet raised all the monuments we need:

Arc de Triomphe, Paris, France

The Arc de Triomphe gets us to see the grandeur of the huge, painful transformation of France during the Revolution. We could do with equally impressive reminders of the grandeur of the present. We need Arcs to *The Heroes of Media Saturation* and *Those Whose Leisure Has Been Sacrificed in the Age of Competition.*

In what ways can you now start to see yourself as a victim of modernity?

In love:

At work:

In family life:

In social life:

In relation to nature:

In your level of anxiety:

19.
Telling the Story of Failure

When we fear failing, we're not only afraid of material cost, we're afraid of humiliation. And what humiliation comes down to often is a way of telling the story of failure.

We need to begin in an odd place, on the steps of the Acropolis:

The Theatre of Dionysus: the birthplace of Greek tragedy

A tragedy is a particular way of telling a story of failure. What is distinctive about tragedy is that the way a story is narrated means that members of the audience typically end up extremely sympathetic towards the failed person. They would never want to call them a loser. That's not how we think of Hamlet or Madame Bovary or Anna Karenina. We call them something far nobler and more admirable: a tragic hero. Tragedy initiates us into a fascinating new concept: *the noble failure*. But we don't usually tell stories of failure like this. Usually, in our society, we tell them via a genre utterly opposed to the subtlety of tragedy – namely, the media. Imagine if some of the greatest stories of tragedy were handled by the media:

Othello: *Love-Crazed Immigrant Kills Senator's Daughter*
Madame Bovary: *Shopaholic Adulteress Swallows Arsenic After Credit Fraud*
Oedipus: *Sex With Mum Was Blinding!*

The headlines sound absurd, but in fact, many of the people we read about in newspapers are treated just as harshly – and yet could be treated as sympathetically as Sophocles' hero.

The trick of living with oneself is to learn to write tragedies like Sophocles or Shakespeare. Not precisely, but in their essence we can learn the underlying attitude of intelligent sympathy that underpins them, and apply this to others and ourselves.

Newspaper exercise

We're all experts at being unbelievably hard on ourselves. Let's perform a little exercise. We could turn all our lives into tabloid fodder, with headlines that make us look like idiots.

Imagine you are working for a big popular newspaper. Turn your life into a harsh headline.

Mummy's Boy With Top Degree Loses Out On Promotion

Loser Still On The Bottom Rung After Seven Years

Deadbeat Can't Get Love Life Together

Then try to retell the same story, not as a lurid headline, but as a story with appropriate sympathy and sadness.

To turn a lurid headline back into the story of a human being, we need to take into account the following:

- full awareness of causes
- impact of family, politics, society
- natural inability to know the future

The moral of the exercise is clear: We need to adjust how we narrate the stories of our own lives.

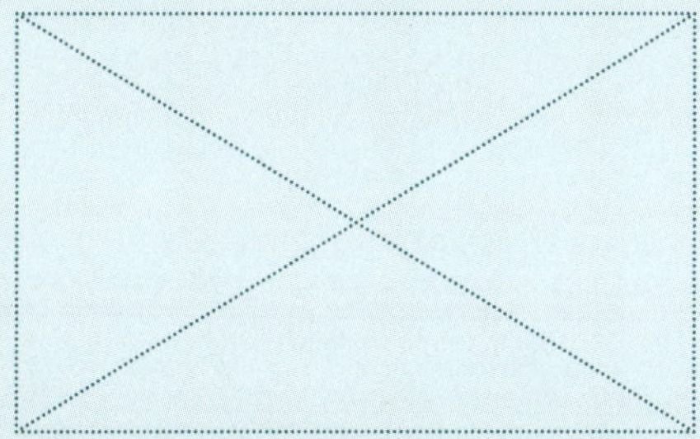

20.
Surrender Expectations

Modern societies continually stress that it is within our powers to achieve a mighty destiny. Whatever the initial hurdles, we can, so the suggestion goes, overcome them all through hard work and the exercise of the will – and thereby forge an exemplary and extraordinary path. We may reach other planets, amass fortunes, run the country, make stunning discoveries in science or produce an outstanding film or novel. We can, through our effort and brilliance, escape the herd. We are surrounded by images of success.

And yet despite all the talk of winning, failure is always the statistical norm. We are far more likely to end up with a mediocre salary, not famous and not especially blessed with looks than we are to end up like the images in the adverts.

We tend to feel a bit sorry for people who play the lottery. We smile at their folly in getting statistics quite so wrong. We think: if they had the wisdom and mathematical intelligence to understand how slim their chances really were, they'd surely never bother. People investing in such slender hopes can appear demented. They are aiming at an impossibly small target.

But most of us are actually no better. We may not have a sense that we're playing any kind of lottery – and yet we are: the lottery of success. We too are clutching tickets of various kinds and setting our sights on statistical near-miracles – even while we think we're being utterly sober, rational and level-headed.

We need to realise we're going to fail almost by definition, and in order to do this, we're going to need to get better at statistics. Let's look at a few.

Chances of starting a billion-dollar company in the USA:	*1 in 785,166 people (0.0001% of the population)*
Chances of earning less than $200,000 per annum in the USA:	*99%*

Number of applicants to Google per year:	*3 million*
Number of employees at Google:	*135,000*
Number of openings per year:	*6,000*
Chances of a job:	*0.2%*

Given the statistics, we should learn a little spoken of art:

There are two ways to feel less of a failure:

1. *On the one hand (and this is very hard), we can try to be more successful.*
2. *On the other (and this can be easier), we can lower the number of things we want to be successful at; we can lower our expectations.*

For the sake of calm – and self-esteem – we need to learn the art of surrendering ambitions. We hear so much about raising ambitions – and yet any good life has to involve their surrender.

It's as important to know how to give up on dreams as it is to create them.

Lowering our expectations sounds like a betrayal of hope. In fact, it can be the beginning of liberation.

Let's listen to William James again:

> *'To give up expectations is as blessed a relief as to get them gratified. There is a strange lightness in the heart when one's nothingness in a particular area is accepted in good faith. How pleasant is the day when we give up striving ... 'Thank God!' we say, 'Those illusions are gone'. Every expectation added to the self is a burden.'*

In the spirit of William James, we now want you to perform an exercise:

Surrendering a dream exercise

Think of one of your very largest dreams, which is proving pretty hard to fulfil.

Write it down on the page provided.

Cut out this page.
Rip it up or burn it.

We don't want to leave it there. We have another idea.

No one succeeds – or fails – at everything.

Every kind of success brings with it a failure in some areas. And the more we can see that our commitment to succeeding at some things has brought failure around other things, the more we can grow at peace.

We are so used to associating the word 'success' with very particular things – status, power and money – that we've failed to notice that the word doesn't cover everything. In the dictionary, success merely means 'excellence in a given field'. At origin, the word is neutral about what it might be applied to. We might, for example, be a success at looking at clouds a lot or saying 'thank you' to strangers. The concept isn't inevitably tied to being a success in the dominant status sense.

We make some key realisations:

No one can ever be a 'success' in every area of life.

We call people 'successes', but we should only ever say 'successes in X or Y area …'

We call people 'failures', but we should only ever say 'failed in X or Y area …'

And success in one area often means failure in another.

For example: a great many people who are immense successes in business also turn out to be great failures with their families. Similarly, many people who are immense successes at family life have not been great successes at corporate culture – for similar reasons. And the great successes at Zen Buddhist contemplation have seldom been great successes at commercial property speculation. Not all 'successes' are compatible with one another. We're always going to need to choose.

Let's look at some of the choices or trade-offs we might be asked to make:

Success in this area …	**… frequently means relative failure in this area**
Climbing the corporate ladder	*Family life*
Family life	*Climbing the corporate ladder*
Philosophy/poetry	*Making money*
Being dependable and methodical	*Taking risks*
Being kind and helpful	*Crushing the competition*
Zen Buddhist detachment	*Commercial property speculation*

The trick is to edge towards success on our own terms. To know what we want to succeed at because we can't succeed at it all …

What trade-offs can we imagine making?

Success in this area …	… frequently means relative failure in this area

21.
Impostor Syndrome

There are times when we are close to an opportunity to do something big, impressive and fulfilling:

- We could join senior management.
- We could start our own business.
- We could create an impressive work of art.
- We could give a really good speech.

And yet we find ourselves feeling fatefully under-confident. We may even turn down the opportunities presented to us because we are crippled by a form of anxiety known as Impostor Syndrome.

Impostor Syndrome is defined as follows: a strong belief that some people are *legitimate* and others are *impostors* – and that we are among the latter, on account of certain things we know about ourselves.

What is it that we are conscious of when we feel like impostors?

When we feel like impostors, we're troubled by a range of weaknesses and fragilities that we know all about within ourselves – but that we don't see any evidence of in other people who are doing what we'd want to do (or are doing).

We are implicitly dividing the world up into two camps – the impostors and the legitimate – and we're placing ourselves with the impostors because of frailties we are very aware of in ourselves.

They are legitimate because ...	**I am an impostor because ...**
They seem confident	*I doubt myself*
They seem sure	*I get anxious*
They seem perfect	*I make mistakes*
They seem calm	*I lose my temper*
They seem normal	*I have weird thoughts*

The problem with Impostor Syndrome is that it involves being grossly unfair to ourselves and grossly over-generous to others. We assume that other people are without errors and frailties while using our errors and frailties as arguments against ourselves. Of course, the truth is that even seemingly legitimate and important people have all the weaknesses and frailties that we have. Why is this so hard to believe? We think there are two reasons:

1. People don't tell us about their frailties

There is a conspiracy of silence about weakness. We know ourselves from the inside, but we know others only from the outside. So we can only know about others from what they opt to disclose. And they don't disclose very much – for the most part. We are left to conclude that we are odder and weaker than everyone else.

Everyone is putting on a 'mask of success'. If we just go by what we publicly know, the mask-like exterior, we may feel that to be a top business person requires a level of invulnerability and strength we don't have.

2. The problem begins in childhood

When we are children, adults seem – on the whole – respectable, powerful and competent. It's normal considering that they've been around for forty years and you're only three years old. They seem not to be worried; they get breakfast every day; they're very knowledgeable; they know how to drive.

Of course, this picture of total competence is false. Everyone remains a 'child' inside, in the sense of being weak, confused, full of oddities and clumsiness. But while we know our child-inside, we don't know other people's.

When we're young, the adults aren't hiding their inner child to be nasty or pretentious; they're just trying to reassure us – but in the process, they give us a distorted image of what it means to be competent. Competence is compatible with remaining – in part – a lost, frightened, intimidated child inside.

To be confident and overcome Impostor Syndrome, we have to perform what we call a 'leap of faith'.

The 16th-century French philosopher Michel de Montaigne is a useful person to think about at this point. He wrote a famous book called *Essays*. In it, he shows a touching awareness of how easy it is to have very low confidence in ourselves. He understood that we can easily think that 'important' or 'esteemed' people don't have all the frailties and weaknesses we have. He wanted to reassure us that – beneath the mask – they do, of course. And he chose to do this via one of the most useful and powerful images of our common vulnerability and humanity: the fact that every day, we have to go and do this very humbling, unimpressive and slightly ridiculous thing, which is defecate.

Montaigne was much more frank. He playfully informed his readers in plain French that:

'Kings and philosophers shit and so do ladies.'

Montaigne knew that for all the evidence of mighty people shitting that exists, we might not guess that this happens at all. But – naturally – it does.

Now by talking about shitting, Montaigne didn't just mean shitting. He was using shitting as representative of a whole host of weaknesses and vulnerabilities we all have. He might have added:

- feeling inadequate
- bumping into doors
- losing one's temper
- having no idea what's going on

And though he was speaking about kings, philosophers and ladies, you can easily add:

- CEOs
- politicians
- successful start-up entrepreneurs
- news anchors

Inner frailties should never have cut us off from doing what impressive people do. These frailties don't make us impostors. They prove our normality and therefore our legitimacy.

Leap of faith exercise

Whenever you feel you are an impostor, remind yourself that the impressive stranger is – despite the lack of surface evidence – just like you in all your frailties. Therefore, nothing fundamental stands between you and the possibility of responsibility, success and fulfilment.

22.
The Call of Death

There is so much that we're anxious about. We're nervous about talking to someone we like the look of ... We're scared of applying for a certain job ... We're too uptight to get down to our work ...

Normally, the way to reassure people is to tell them that everything is going to be OK if they do take a risk and move forward. This is not quite our way.

We want to frighten you into confidence. We want to make you more scared of some things, so that you can be less scared of others.

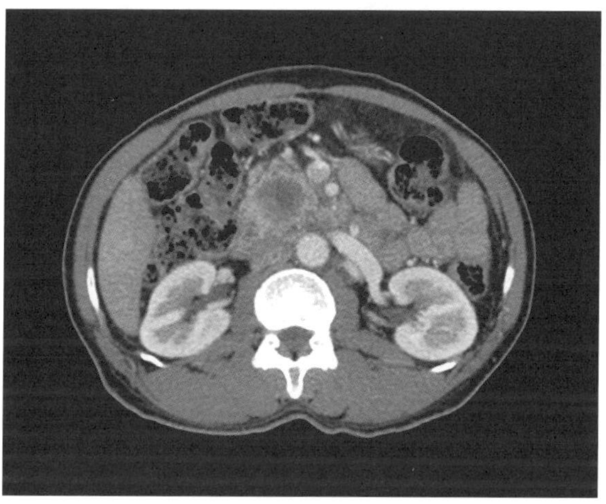

A diagnosis like this can put our everyday fears and worries into perspective.

This is a CT scan through someone with advanced pancreatic cancer. Generally, people only discover pancreatic cancer when the tumour is already well developed. Not that that really matters, because pancreatic cancer typically has a very low survival rate. You'll likely be gone within six months – maybe if you're really lucky, a year. And it will probably spread, usually to your lungs and throat, making it difficult to breathe and swallow. It is appalling – and it is real. The rest of us will go from a combination of heart attacks, liver cancers, brain tumours and Alzheimer's

– among others. So we need to get things in perspective.

This is not frightening:

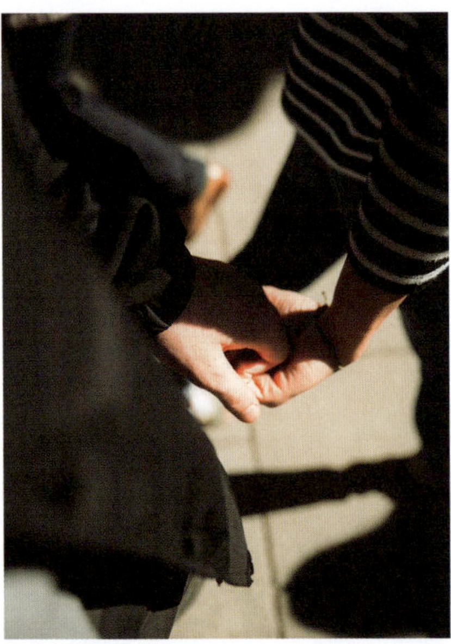

This is nothing to be scared of.

It's not frightening to dare to ask to touch someone's hand, or to get their number, or to ask for a job. In comparison with our final exit, the pains and troubles of our bolder moves and riskier ventures do not, in the end, have to be terrifying.

With that in mind, in very simple words …

Go and do it. We each know what *it* is …

What do you need to do next …?

23.
Ecce Homo

From time to time we all feel inadequate about ourselves and our endeavours. The German philosopher Friedrich Nietzsche knew this very well; he was acutely aware of the crippling effects of low self-esteem. His books were frequently slated by reviewers and his supporters were few. He would not, however, let himself be dragged down by these circumstances, but composed an antidote in the form of an autobiography, *Ecce Homo* (*Behold, The Man*). It is an extraordinary exercise in how to buoy up one's self-confidence without becoming puffed up.

The procedure of Ecce Homo is simple: examine your life dispassionately. This is a difficult thing to do. Either we remember only the good bits and so develop an inflated, unrealistic sense of our abilities, or we remember only the bad incidents and become ever more morose. Nietzsche focuses attention in surprising places. He is proud of the fact that he moved from Germany to Italy because the weather is better there. Normally we don't see that as an achievement, but he sees that it was a big thing for him to realise that rain and cloudy days got him down and to do something about it. He is proud of the music he likes (Rossini, Chopin), even though these were hardly unusual preferences at the time. He likes that he has worked out who his favourite writers are: Montaigne and Molière. He has stopped drinking beer; he has lightened his diet. He is ready to chalk up as successes things which are really good in his life, even though they may not look particularly impressive to anyone else.

All this could sound trivial, but Nietzsche has latched onto a real problem. For decent, sensitive people it can be remarkably hard to appreciate oneself. And this difficulty undermines self-confidence. We find it hard to form a just opinion of our own merits. We are so used to the problem of people having too high an opinion of themselves that we naturally forget the reverse (but for many people very real) difficulty of not thinking well enough of oneself.

So often self-confidence is dependent on the basic but – for good people – elusive premise: I'm fine as I am.

Imagine that you are fine as you are. What about your life is – actually – OK?

24.
You are 'Good Enough'

The mid-20th-century English psychoanalyst Donald Winnicott, who specialised in working with parents and children, was disturbed by how often he encountered in his consulting rooms parents who were deeply disappointed with themselves. They felt they were failing as parents and hated themselves intensely as a result. They were ashamed of their occasional rows, their bursts of short temper, their times of boredom around their own children and their many mistakes. They were haunted by a range of anxious questions: are we too strict, too lenient, too protective, not protective enough? What struck Winnicott, however, was that these people were almost always not at all bad parents. They were loving, often very kind, very interested in their children; they tried hard to meet their needs and to understand their problems as best they could. As parents, they were – as he came to put it in a hugely memorable and important phrase – 'good enough'.

Winnicott was putting a finger on a crucial issue. We often torment ourselves because we have in our minds a very demanding – and, in fact, impossible – vision of what we're supposed to be like across a range of areas of our lives. This vision doesn't emerge from a careful study of what actual people are like. Instead, it's a fantasy, a punitive perfectionism, drawn from the cultural ether.

When it comes to parenting, we imagine a fantasy of parents who are always calm, always perfectly wise, always there when their child needs them. There are no parents like this. But a Romantic conception of the perfect parent can fill our minds and make us deeply anxious and fretful – because our own family life inevitably looks so messy and muddled by comparison. Astonishingly and unreasonably inflated expectations leave us only able to perceive where we have fallen short.

With the phrase 'good enough', Winnicott was initiating a hugely important project. He wanted to move us away from idealisation. Ideals may sound nice, but they bring a terrible problem in their wake: they can make us despair of the merely quite good things we already do and have. 'Good enough' is a cure for the sickness of idealisation.

Winnicott introduced the idea of 'good enough' around parenting. But it applies widely across our lives – because we idealise cruelly around a great many different things. For example, we might refer to the 'good enough job'. It may not meet our fantasy demands: creative yet secure, fascinating yet unstressful, morally uplifting yet highly paid. But by the standards of what real jobs are like, it might be rather OK and worth taking pride in. Or we could speak of the 'good enough marriage'. It might not be the perfect union of two souls; sex may be intermittent; there may be regular frustrations and misunderstandings and a fair number of flare-ups. But by the standards of actual long-term relationships, that might be genuine success.

By dialling down our expectations, the idea of 'good enough' resensitises us to the lesser – but very real – virtues we already possess, but which our unreal hopes have made us overlook.

A 'good enough' life is not a bad life. It's the best existence that actual humans are ever likely to lead.

In what ways are you a good enough lover?

In what ways are you a good enough friend?

In what ways are you a good enough parent?

In what ways are you a good enough human?

25.
Inner Voices

In our minds, we all have inner voices. They talk to us as we try to achieve things or deal with our lives. Sometimes they are kind voices: they say, 'Go on, you can do it.' Sometimes, they are punitive voices: 'You little idiot,' they say.

An important part of calming ourselves involves auditing these voices – working out whose voices they are and then sorting out which voices we really want to keep in our minds.

The origins of our inner voices are basic: they are an internalisation of the voices of people who were once outside us. We absorb the tones of indifference, charity, contempt or warmth that we will have heard across our formative years.

An inner voice is an outer voice that we have – imperceptibly – made our own. We've absorbed the tone of a kind and gentle caregiver who liked to laugh indulgently at our foibles and had endearing names for us. Or else the voice of a harassed or angry parent; the menacing threats of an elder sibling keen to put us down; the words of a schoolyard bully or a teacher who seemed impossible to please.

We take in these voices because at certain key moments in the past they sounded so compelling and irresistible. The dominant past figures repeated their messages over and over until they got lodged in our own way of thinking – for better or for worse.

Let us try to audit some of our inner voices and also try to imagine how we might speak to ourselves differently.

An Inner Voice Audit

Situation	Something I'd probably say to myself	Who from my past does this sound a bit like?
I've put off something and now have to do it in a panicked rush	*Never ever keep people waiting*	*Father*
The hotel isn't as nice as it should be		
I get feedback that's a bit critical		
It's a beautiful sunny day		
The government is in trouble		
I think of an intense sexual fantasy		
I succeed		
I realise I've offended someone		
I tried to seduce someone – and failed		

Is this voice kindly/ constructive/supportive? Yes/No	The ideal person who might speak to me at this point	What they might say
No	*Grandmother /Montaigne*	*There's always time*

We do have leeway in how we speak to ourselves. One approach is to identify a nice voice we knew in the past and give it more scope. Perhaps there was a kindly grandparent who was quick to see our side of things and who would offer us deft words of encouragement. If we knocked our orange juice all over the carpet they'd remind us that accidents can happen to everyone (last week they themselves spilt a cup of coffee over the sofa). Instead of promoting a punitive, critical voice, they represent a calm, understanding way of addressing failings. We can try to focus on this kind of supportive approach and summon it on a regular basis; rather than waiting for it to pop (as it rarely does) into our heads, we can deliberately nurture and train it.

A good internal voice is rather like (and just as important as) a genuinely decent judge; someone who needs to be there to separate good from bad but who can always be merciful, fair, accurate in understanding what's going on and interested in helping us deal with our problems. It's not that we should stop judging ourselves, rather that we should learn to be better judges of ourselves.

The other major strategy for changing the voices in our heads is to try to become an imaginary friend to ourselves. This sounds odd initially because we naturally imagine a friend as someone else, not as a part of our own mind. But there is value in the concept because of the extent to which we know how to treat our friends with a sympathy and imagination we don't apply to ourselves. If a friend is in trouble our first instinct is rarely to tell them that they are fundamentally an idiot or a failure. If a friend complains that their partner isn't very warm to them, we don't tell them they're getting what they deserve. In friendship, we know instinctively how to deploy strategies of wisdom and consolation that we stubbornly refuse to apply to ourselves.

The good friend is compassionate. When we fail, as we will, they are understanding and generous around our mishaps. Our folly doesn't exclude us from the circle of their love. The good friend deftly conveys that to err is what we humans do. They're continually telling us that our specific case might be unique but that the general structure is common. People don't just sometimes fail. Everyone fails, only we don't know about it.

We do actually already possess the relevant skills of friendship, it's just we haven't as yet directed them to the person who probably needs them most – namely, of course, ourselves.

If you were a better friend to yourself ...

What would you tell yourself about your failures?

What would you tell yourself about your ambitions?

How would you consider what you have been through till now?

26.
Remaining Calm around Other People

Other people are, of course, frequently extremely annoying.

Annoying people in your life	Annoying things they do/have done

One of the most fundamental paths to calm is the power to hold on, even in very challenging situations, to a distinction between what someone does and what they *meant to do.*

When trying to explore why the people who annoy us behaved as they did, we tend to use some stock explanations, defined in the left-hand column of the table overleaf.

Write down some annoying people in your life that seem to match these explanations:

Reasons why people do bad things	Annoying people in my life
They're evil	
They're thoughtless	
They're selfish	
They're deluded	
They're unkind	
They're narcissistic	
They're mad	
They're out to get me	

It's very understandable that we often ascribe very negative intentions to people who frustrate us. But is it fair or helpful?

Small children sometimes behave in stunningly unfair and shocking ways: they scream at the person who is looking after them, angrily push away a bowl of pasta, throw away something one has just fetched for them. But we are able not to feel agitated or personally wounded by their actions.

The reason is that we don't at once assign a negative motive or mean intention to their behaviour. We reach around for the most benevolent interpretations we can pull together. We don't immediately presume that the child is proving maddening in order to upset us. We probably think:

- They are getting a bit tired.
- Their gums are sore.
- They are upset by the arrival of a younger sibling.

We have a repertoire of alternative explanations ready in our heads to take the edge off an unappealing trait – and none of these leads us to panic or gets us terribly agitated.

This is the reverse of what tends to happen around adults. Here we imagine that others have deliberately got us in their sights:

- If our partner is late for our mother's birthday because of 'work', we may assume it's an excuse.
- If a friend promised to buy us some extra toothpaste but then 'forgot', we'll imagine a deliberate slight.
- If a colleague is in a bad mood, we think they are attempting to ruin our lives.

We have a rather odd-sounding suggestion: we should – sometimes, within reason – learn to look at other people as if they were small children.

Reasons (we think) children behave badly:	Reasons (we think) adults behave badly:	Reasons why adults behave badly:
They're tired.	*They're trying to hurt us.*	*They're tired.*
They're hungry.	*They're evil.*	*They're hungry.*
They need a hug.	*They're stupid.*	*They need a hug.*
Someone else hurt them.	*They're being vengeful.*	*Someone else hurt them.*
They're scared.	*They're being malicious.*	*They're scared.*
They need some attention.	*They're narcissistic.*	*They need some attention.*
They can't explain what's really bothering them.	*They're idiots.*	*They can't explain what's really bothering them.*

Even though someone might be six feet tall and have a beard, or hold down a job as a corporate lawyer, there are many ways in which the adult mind is very similar to – and no more evil than – that of a 3-year-old. We too are afraid, tired, anxious and in need of a hug – and this is what makes us behave badly.

What that means in practice is that we must look beneath and beyond a fellow adult's rather disappointing surface behaviour and search for reasons for it that are forgiving:

- Maybe they're tired.
- Maybe they're disappointed with themselves.

There are obviously ways of exaggerating this: we are not recommending the tolerance of abuse. We're pointing out a path to a kind of love we will have to show in order to make love work in the long term.

It's very touching that we live in a world where we have learnt to be so kind to children; it would be even nicer if we learnt to be a little more generous towards the childlike parts of one another.

Part of the reason why we jump so readily to dark conclusions and see plots to insult and harm us is that poignant psychological phenomenon: self-hatred. The less we are inclined to see ourselves with compassion, the less we are likely to extend that compassion towards others. Instead, we see others' negative behaviour not as a sign that they might be struggling, but as something we deserve. When we carry an excess of self-disgust around with us, operating just below the radar of conscious awareness, we'll constantly seek confirmation from the wider world that we really are the worthless people we take ourselves to be.

The expectation is almost always set in childhood, where someone close to us is likely to have left us feeling ashamed and culpable – and as a result, we now travel through society assuming the worst, not because it is necessarily true (or pleasant) to do so, but because it feels familiar; because we are the prisoners of past patterns we haven't yet understood.

The French philosopher Émile-Auguste Chartier (known as Alain) was said to be the finest teacher in France in the first half of the 20th century. He developed a formula for calming himself and his pupils down in the face of irritating people. 'Never say that people are evil,' he wrote. 'You just need to look for the pin.'

What he meant was: look for the source of the agony that drives a person to behave in appalling ways. The calming thought is to imagine that they are suffering off-stage, in some area we cannot see. To be mature is to learn to imagine this zone of pain, in spite of the lack of much available evidence. They may not look as if they were maddened by an inner psychological ailment; they may look chirpy and full of themselves. But the 'pin' simply must be there – or they would not be causing us harm.

We need to imagine the turmoil, disappointment, worry and sadness in people who may outwardly appear merely aggressive. We need to aim compassion at an unexpected place: those who annoy us most.

Pin exercise

Revisit the list of annoying people in your life. Then try to think of the real, deep reason why they behave as they do. See if you can move from frustration to pity.

People who annoy me	What might be the pin?

27.
Care around the News

We know that we must, to lay claim to any respectability or competence, keep up with the news. That's why we've ringed the Earth with satellites, criss-crossed it with fibre-optic cables and created networks of bureaus that inform us with maniacal urgency of pretty much any event to have unfolded anywhere on the planet in the last few moments. We are, furthermore, equipped with tiny devices that we keep very close to hand, and which we tend to check at intervals of between one and five minutes (rarely longer) to monitor all unfolding stories in close to real time. We have been granted a ringside seat on the second-by-second flow of history.

What are the big stories that are dominating the news now?

1.

2.

3.

As a result of our immersion in news, we see a lot more. And at the same time, strangely, we see a lot less. The constant presence of news from without hampers our ability to pick up on an equally important, though far less prestigious source of news from within.

We are not, by nature, well equipped to see inside ourselves. Consciousness bobs like a small boat on a sea of disavowed emotions. A lot of feelings and ideas require a high degree of courage to confront. They threaten to make us uncomfortably anxious, excited or sad were we to learn more about them. So we use the news without to silence the news from within. We have the most prestigious excuse ever invented never to spend any time roaming freely inside our own minds. It is not that the news from without is unimportant to someone (indeed, it will be the most important thing in certain people's lives a continent away, or in a company in the capital, or somewhere in the upper reaches of government); it's just that this news is almost certainly wholly disconnected from our real priority over the coming years, which is to make the most of our life and our talents in the time that remains to us. It is touching that we should give so much of our curiosity over to strangers, but it is poignant that we are forced eventually to pay such a high price for this constant dispersal of energy. We dismiss fragile, tentative thoughts about what we should do next, who we should call, what we really need to do – thoughts upon which an adequate future for us depends – for the sake of the more obvious drama of the moment. But the drama won't save us, and cares not a jot about our development or our real responsibilities.

Our news organisations constantly update us about the most dramatic events unfolding right now – which they mischievously encourage us to confuse with what it might be most productive for us to know about in the coming minutes. However, there is an easily missed but radical difference between 'novelty' and 'importance': what is new is not necessarily vital for us to think about, and what we should really listen to might be news that's far more familiar to us. For example, what we might actually have to fill our minds with – and what would thereby legitimately merit the term 'news' – might not be another scandal in politics or last night's sporting victory, but a thought about our relationship or our career.

It feels counter-intuitive to think that there might be certain things more important than the news. But there are: our own lives, which we have ever more respectable reasons to avoid confronting.

What are the big stories that should be dominating *your life* now, but can be hard to think about?

1.

2.

3.

28.
History and the News

We tend to get very gloomy and worried about our own era: the state of society seems especially lamentable; the international situation is dire; the political process is unnerving; commercial society is rapacious; the media is hysterical and vulgar; education is in crisis. We feel we are living in terrible times. But 'terrible' in comparison to what? The media constantly invites us to view how things are today against a very narrow slice of time. Things feel worse than they were yesterday or last week or two years ago – before the most recent atrocity, economic downturn or security crisis.

What feels worse than ever to you?

....

....

....

....

....

....

By contrast, what we call 'history' offers us a much bigger, fairer and more consoling comparison across large slices of time. It frames what is happening now against the perspective of how things normally tend to go over decades and centuries.

It teaches us some usefully dark lessons. We learn that societies are rarely very admirable; there are always crises; economies pretty much always fluctuate; manners and morals are always shifting and in some ways getting worse; almost no human communities have ever been remarkably just or equal; progressive moments never quite achieve what was hoped of them and are almost always followed by periods of reaction. Nevertheless, history also reminds us that things have seemed close to outright collapse many times before, but that eventually humanity has more or less pulled through. The Roman Empire was governed for many years by a string of horrendous emperors like Nero and Caligula. But this didn't signal the end of everything, as it must on some days have seemed like it must. The chaotic years were followed a bit later by a succession of able and honourable governments (including that of the philosopher Marcus Aurelius) and long periods of civilised prosperity. The troubles of our own times are – much more than we tend to suppose – at once very normal and much less fatal than we are inclined to imagine.

The news is always trying to stoke our natural panic – for its own commercial ends (there is no money to be made reassuring audiences that things will, on measure, be OK). By contrast, history is like the person who has been on rough seas for many years and can compare any one storm with a great many others. History is an artificial, laboriously constructed, beautiful corrective to the natural, short-term perspectives of our timid, jumpy minds.

Genuinely awful things are compatible with a society heading overall towards peace and prosperity. It is not fatal for societies to be in trouble; it is usual for things to go rather badly. In this respect, reading ancient history generates the opposite emotions to scanning today's news. The news machine is based on the idea of getting us agitated. News is always trying to tell us that something entirely new and very alarming is occurring: there's a wholly original health risk, international conflict, threat to global stability or risk to the economy. But history knows that news has been much worse before and things were, in the end, OK. People behaving very badly is a normal state of affairs. It was ever thus: there have always been disappointing leaders and greedy magnates. There have always been existential threats to the human race and civilisation. It makes no sense, and is a form of twisted narcissism, to imagine that our era has any kind of monopoly on perversity or chaos.

On a grand scale, this explains why grandparents typically have a calmer approach to bringing up children than parents do. The grandparents have a more accurate grasp of how normal – and therefore less alarming – many problems are. Their calm is based on two key bits of knowledge. They know that whatever is done, one's children will turn out very far from perfect – and therefore the intensely agitating worry that one might be making a mistake is usually a bit misplaced. But they also grasp that even when things go a bit wrong, children will generally cope well enough. Their sense of danger and their sense of hope have both been made more accurate by experience. History encourages the less panicky sides of ourselves.

Take what you have written on page 167 and turn it into a few sentences in a history book written in 2193.

29.
No One Is Normal

Most of us are rather interested in being normal – but are very anxious that we're not.

In what areas might I be a bit odd?

Area of oddity	What makes me odd

We want so much to belong and be 'sane' – and yet we worry a lot about ways in which we don't quite and aren't. No matter how much we praise individualism and celebrate ourselves as unique, we are, in many areas, deeply concerned with fitting in.

But the good news is that our picture of what is normal is, in fact – very often – way out of line with what is actually true and widespread. Many things that we might assume to be uniquely odd or disconcertingly strange about us are in reality completely average and ubiquitous, though simply rarely spoken of in the reserved and cautious public sphere.

The idea of the normal currently in circulation is not an accurate map of what is actually customary for a human being. We are – each one of us – far more compulsive, anxious, sexual, high-minded, mean, generous, playful, thoughtful, dazed and at sea than we are ever encouraged to admit.

Part of the reason for our misunderstanding of our normality comes down to a basic fact about our minds: that we know through immediate experience what is going on inside us, but can only know about other people from what they choose to tell us – which will almost always be a very edited version of the truth. We know what we've done at 3 a.m., but we imagine others sleeping peacefully. We know our somewhat shocking desires from close up, but we are left to guess about other people's from what their faces tell us, which is not very much.

This asymmetry between self-knowledge and knowledge-of-others is what lies behind loneliness. We simply can't trust that our deep selves can have counterparts in those we meet, and so we stay silent and isolated. The asymmetry encourages shyness too, for we struggle to believe that the imposing, competent strangers we encounter can have any of the vulnerabilities and idiocies we're so intimately familiar with inside our own characters.

We are particularly bad at recognising how normal it is to suffer and to be unhappy. Around relationships, for example, we constantly operate with an image of the bliss of others which mocks and undermines our own efforts to keep going with many flawed but eminently 'good enough' unions. We find it hard to bear in mind that more or less everyone is, beneath a cheery surface, intermittently profoundly sad and rarely not anxious. We become embarrassed too by our close-up knowledge of our own sexuality, which appears necessarily more perverse than that of anyone we know. It almost certainly isn't. We simply haven't been told the full story.

Our culture often tries to project an idea of an organised, poised and polished self, as the standard way most people are. We should discount any such myth. Other people are always far more likely to be as we know we are – with all our quirks, fragilities, compulsions and surprising aspects – than they are to be like the apparently 'normal' types we meet in social life.

Go back to the chart you filled out on the previous page.

Cross out the heading 'What makes me odd' and replace it with 'What makes me normal'.

30.
A Quiet Life

Many of us feel restless from a sense that a better life is going on elsewhere. We suffer from the fear of missing out (FOMO). The catalysts of FOMO are everywhere. We're continually being bombarded with suggestions about what we might do (try the new restaurant in town, buy tickets to the latest show, study abroad, go on holiday) or where the really extraordinary parties, cities and jobs might be. The modern world makes sure we know at all times just how much fun and interest is unfolding elsewhere. It is a culture in which intense and painful doses of FOMO are almost inevitable.

What might you be missing out on?

....

....

....

....

....

....

There are, fundamentally, two ways in which the brute facts of missing out can be viewed: one can take a Romantic or a Classical approach. To the Romantic temperament, missing out causes immense agony. Somewhere else, noble and interesting and attractive people are living exactly the life that should be ours. We'd be so happy, if only we could be over there, at that party, with those people, or working for that company in New York City, or holidaying on that beach in Spain. Sometimes it may make us want to burst into tears. The Romantic believes in the idea of a defined centre where the most exciting things are happening. For a few years it was Berlin, then London. Now, it's probably San Francisco and in five years it may be Auckland – or perhaps Rio. For the Romantic, humanity is divided into a large group of the mediocre and a tribe of the elect: artists, entrepreneurs, the edgy part of the fashion world and the people doing creative things with tech. As a Romantic, it can be exhausting inside our soul. Our mother sometimes drives us to fury: Her life is utterly dull. How can she accept it? Why isn't she itching to move to the Bay Area? She's always suggesting we take a job closer to her, or inviting us on walking holidays in the Lake District. Sometimes we are quite rude to her.

For their part, Classically minded people acknowledge that there are, of course, some genuinely marvellous things going on in the world, but they doubt that the obvious signs of glamour are a good guide to finding them. The best novel in the world, they like to think, is probably not currently winning prizes or storming up the bestseller lists. It may be being written at this moment by an arthritic woman living in the otherwise unremarkable Latvian town of Liepāja. Classical people are intensely aware that good qualities coexist with some extremely ordinary ones. Everything is rather jumbled up. Lamentable taste in jumpers is compatible with extraordinary insight. Academic qualifications can give no indication of true intelligence. Famous people can be dull. Obscure ones can be remarkable. At a perfect launch party, drinking sandalwood cocktails at the coolest bar in the world, one could feel sad and anxious. One might have the deepest conversations of one's life with an aunt – even though she likes watching snooker on television and has stopped dyeing her hair. The Classical temperament also fears missing out but has a rather different list of things they are afraid of not enjoying: getting to truly know one's parents; learning to cope well with being alone; appreciating the consoling power of trees and clouds; discovering what their favourite pieces of music really mean to them; chatting to a 7-year-old child … As these wise souls know, one can indeed miss out on some extremely important things if one is always rushing a little too intently to find excitement elsewhere. They are enthusiastic advocates of a quiet life.

A quiet life sounds like an option that only the defeated would ever be inclined to praise. The age is overwhelmingly alive to the benefits of active, social, complex and ambitious ways of living. Lauding a quiet life has some of the eccentricity of praising rain.

We are suspicious because the defenders of quiet lives have so often come from the most implausible sections of the community: slackers, hippies, the work-shy … those who seem like they never had a choice; people whose quiet lives appear to have been imposed upon them by their own ineptitude.

And yet, when we examine things further, busy lives turn out to have so many incidental costs that we have been collectively committed to ignoring.

At the top, alongside our privileges, we may grow impoverished in curious ways. Our every word may be listened to with trembling respect within a vast organisation, but what we absolutely cannot do is admit that we are also extremely tired and simply want to spend the afternoon reading on the sofa. We grow to be strangers to those who love us outside of our wealth and status – while depending ever more on the fickle attention of those for whom we are our achievements alone. Our children see ever less of us. Our spouses grow bitter.

We are at this point in history so deeply fixated on the idea that poverty must always be involuntary and therefore the result of lack of talent and indigence that we have trouble imagining that it might be the result of an intelligent and skilled person's free choice based on a rational evaluation of costs and benefits. It might sincerely be possible for someone to decide not to take the better-paid job, not because they had no chance, but because – having surveyed the externalities involved – they did not think it worth it.

When we come to know the true price some ways of life exact, we may slowly realise we are not willing to pay for the envy, fear, deceit and anxiety. Our days are limited on the Earth. We may – for the sake of true riches – willingly, and with no loss of dignity, opt to become a little more reclusive, temperate and obscure.

How could my life be quieter?

....

....

....

What might I enjoy in a quieter life?

....

....

....

....

31.
Small Pleasures

Small pleasures – such as a warm bath, a slice of fresh bread, a conversation with a close friend or a good night of sleep – lack prestige or social support. Our age believes in big pleasures. We've developed a suspicion of the ordinary (which is taken to be mediocre, dull and uninspiring) and work with a corresponding assumption that things that are unique, hard to find, exotic or unfamiliar are naturally fitted to delight us more. We subtly like high prices. If something is cheap or free, it's a little harder to appreciate. We are mostly focused on large schemes that we hope will deliver substantial enjoyment: marriage, career, travel and the purchase of a house.

The approach isn't wholly wrong, but unwittingly it exhibits a vicious and unhelpful bias against the cheap, the easily available, the ordinary, the familiar and the small scale.

Yet the paradoxical aspect of pleasure is how promiscuous it proves to be. It doesn't neatly collect in the most expensive boutiques. It can refuse to stick with us on grand holidays. It is remarkably vulnerable to emotional trouble, sulks and casual bad moods.

A pleasure may look very minor – eating a fig, whispering in bed in the dark, talking to a grandparent or scanning through old photos – and yet be anything but. If properly grasped and elaborated upon, these sorts of activities may be among the most moving and satisfying we can have.

Appreciating what is to hand isn't a defence of failure; it isn't an attack on ambition. But there is no point in chasing the future until and unless we are attuned to the modest moments and things that are available to us already.

The smallness of a pleasure isn't really an assessment of how much it has to offer us; it is a reflection of how many good things the world unfairly neglects. A small pleasure is a great pleasure in waiting; it is a true source of joy which has not yet received the collective acknowledgement it is due.

My small pleasures

Remind yourself of your small pleasures – and give them weight in your life.

Small pleasure	Degree of pleasure out of 10	Price

32.
Teasing Oneself

One way to remain calm is to remember regularly to tease oneself.

Teasing done with affection and skill is a profound human accomplishment. There's nasty teasing, of course, in which we pick away at a sore spot in someone's life or mock our own beings. But there is a genuinely valuable affectionate version, generous and loving, which feels good to be on the receiving end of.

All of us get a bit unbalanced in one way or another: too serious, too gloomy, too jokey. And so we all benefit from being tugged back towards a healthier mean by a well-aimed, tenderly delivered tease. The good teaser latches on to and responds to our distinctive quirks and gets compassionately constructive about trying to reconnect us with our better selves, not by delivering a stern lesson, but by helping us to notice our excesses and laugh at them. We sense the teaser trying – with love – to give us a useful small shove in a good (and secretly welcome) direction.

The best teasing remarks emerge from genuine insights into who we are. A person has studied us, put their finger on a struggle that's going on in us and has taken the part of the highest – but currently under-supported – side of us. This feels so good because, only too often, others simply don't see past the forbidding or off-putting front we end up putting on for the world; they have no imagination to detect the kinder self beneath the tricky surface. They simply think we are gloomy, stern, angry or obsessed. The teaser does us the favour of recognising that the dominant front isn't telling the whole story.

Teasing is a subtle, powerful mode of teaching. It builds on a hugely important insight about human beings: criticism of any kind is exceptionally hard to absorb; we are very slow and reluctant learners, with well-observed tendencies to ignore and turn against those who try to lecture us. By amusingly exaggerating our exaggerations, teasing combines criticism with charm; the negative point is real, but it is carefully wrapped in kindness and disguised as mere entertainment – and is therefore much easier to take on board. It seduces us into virtue. As George Bernard Shaw knew, 'If you want to tell people the truth, make them laugh, otherwise they'll kill you.'

Self-teasing exercise

What faults might you be teased about?

What might be funny about them?

How might you have a laugh with yourself about yourself?

33.
Keeping Faith with 'Rupture' and 'Repair'

Many of the moments in which we lose our sense of calm are when we perceive something to be broken – a bond of trust or an easy relationship with someone we believe can be kind and understanding of our needs. At times like this we might usefully look at tensions within our friendships and relationships through the prism of a concept much used within psychotherapy: the idea of 'rupture' and 'repair'.

For psychotherapists, every relationship is at risk of moments of frustration, or as the term has it, of 'rupture'.

The ruptures can often be quite small, and to outside observers perhaps imperceptible: one person fails to respond warmly to another's greeting; someone tries to explain an idea to a friend who shrugs and says off-handedly that they have no idea what they're on about; in front of colleagues, a lover shares an anecdote which casts the partner in a less than flattering light. Or the rupture can be more serious: someone calls someone else a stupid fool and breaks a door. A birthday is forgotten. An affair begins.

The point about ruptures is that they say nothing – in themselves – about a friendship or relationship's prospects of survival. There might be constant rather grave ruptures and no break-up. Or there might be one or two tense moments over a minor disagreement – and things head towards collapse.

What determines the difference is something that psychotherapists are especially keen to teach us about: the capacity for what they term 'repair'. Repair refers to the work needed for two people to regain each other's trust, and restore themselves in the other's mind as someone who is essentially decent and sympathetic and can be a 'good enough' interpreter of their needs. As psychotherapy points out, repair isn't just one capacity among others; it is arguably the central determinant of one's mastery of emotional maturity; it is what identifies us as true adults.

Good repair relies on at least four separate skills:

1. The ability to apologise

A sorry may not be as easy as it sounds, for it isn't just a few warm words one has to say – the true cost is to one's self-love. If one is already on the verge of finding oneself somewhat intolerable, then the call to concede yet another point – to own up to being still more foolish, emotionally unbalanced, controlling, hot-tempered or vain – can feel like a demand too far. We may opt to dig in and avoid a sorry not because we are overly pleased with ourselves, but precisely because our unworthiness feels so painfully obvious to us already – and lends us no faith to imagine that any apologies we did make could arouse the kind of forbearance and kindness we crave – and yet so badly feel we don't deserve.

2. The ability to forgive

There can be equal difficulty around being able to accept an apology. To do so requires us to extend imaginative sympathy for why good people (which includes us) can end up doing some pretty bad things, not because they are 'evil', but because they are in their varied ways tired or sad, worried or weak. A forgiving outlook lends us energy to look around for the most generous reasons why fundamentally decent people can at points behave less than optimally.

When this kind of forgiveness feels impossible, therapists speak of a manoeuvre of the mind known as 'splitting', a tendency to declare some people to be entirely good and others, just as simply, entirely awful. In dividing humanity like this, we protect ourselves from what can feel like the impossible dangers of disappointment or grown-up ambivalence. Either someone is pure and perfect and we can love them without reserve or – quite suddenly – they must be appalling and we can never ever forgive them. We might cling to rupture because it confirms a story which, though deeply sad at one level, also feels very safe: that big emotional commitments are invariably too risky, that others can't be trusted, that hope is an illusion – and that we are basically all alone.

3. The ability to teach

Behind a rupture, there often lies a failed attempt by one person to teach something to another. There was something that they were trying to get across when they lost their temper or got into a sulk – something about how to behave around a parent or what to do about sex, how to approach childcare or how to handle money. And yet the effort went wrong and they forgot all about the art of good teaching – an art which relies, to a surprising extent, on a degree of pessimism about the ability of another person to understand what we want from them.

Good teachers know how resistant the human mind can be to new ideas. They don't shout, because they didn't from the outset allow themselves to believe in total symmetries of mind. They don't push a point too hard, but give their listener time. They know about defensiveness – and as a fallback, accept that they may have to respect two different realities. They can, in the end, bear to accept that they will always be a bit misunderstood even by someone who loves them very much.

4. The ability to learn

It can feel so much easier to get offended with someone than to dare to imagine that they might have something important to tell us. We may prefer to get hung up about how they informed us of an idea, rather than address the substance of what they are trying to convey. It isn't easy to accept that we might not be getting it right and that we are still beginners in a range of areas. The good repairer is ultimately a good learner: they have a lively and non-humiliating sense of how much they still have left to take on board. It isn't a surprise or a cause for alarm that someone might level a criticism at them; it's merely a sign that a kindly soul is invested enough in their development to notice areas of immaturity – and, in the safety of a relationship, to offer them something almost no one otherwise ever bothers with: feedback.

It is no doubt a fine thing to have friendships and relationships without moments of rupture, but it is an even finer and nobler achievement to know how to patch things up repeatedly with those precious strands of emotional gold: self-acceptance, patience, humility, courage and a lot of tenderness.

With reference to the ideas here, imagine how you might patch things up with key people in your life.

Person I had a rupture with	What might have been going on for them?	What was I trying to tell them?

What were they trying to tell me?	How might I repair the friendship/relationship?

34.
Cheerful Despair

One of philosophy's most established oppositions, depicted in art throughout the centuries, is between two great Greek thinkers, Democritus and Heraclitus. Both men (who lived to a very old age) had a deep knowledge of people and the world, but responded to what they knew in strikingly different ways. Heraclitus could not stop weeping; Democritus could not stop laughing.

Peter Paul Rubens, *Heraclitus and Democritus*, 1603

We might understand why there was cause for Heraclitus to weep, but what of Democritus? Crucially, Democritus laughed not because a privileged position led him naïvely to misunderstand how bad things could be. His good humour wasn't a version of sentimentality or avoidant optimism. Nor was it simply a random quirk of temperament. Democritus laughed in a very particular and admirable way because he had learnt the subtle art of Cheerful Despair.

The philosopher recommended that we acquaint ourselves with the totality of human experience, with all its failings, follies, self-deception and casual (and not so casual) injustices. The wise person should take care to grow completely at home with the ordinary shambles of existence. They must never be taken by surprise or shocked by how things can be, for they have taken full notice of the facts and so can be embittered by nothing. Betrayal, murder, sexual deviance, corruption – all are already factored in. The wise understand that they are living on a dunghill. When baseness and malice rear their heads, as they will, it is against a backdrop of fully vanquished hope, and so there will be no sense of having been unfairly let down and having had one's credulity betrayed. Democritus was so convinced of the darkness, he no longer had to register it constantly at the front of his mind in order to do it justice. It seemed an entirely obvious, baseline fact about existence.

The laughing Greek could be cheerful because anything nice, sweet or charming that came his way was immediately experienced as a bonus, a deeply gratifying addition to his original bleak premises. By keeping the dark backdrop of life always in mind, he sharpened his appreciation of whatever stood out against it. He did not have to be on constant high alert for the negative; he had the inner space to listen out for the faintest signals of redemption. The positive was not a feeble echo of dashed hopes; it was a particularly delightful, slightly improbable but noteworthy bucking of the usual and expected tragic trend.

Democritus was known to be fond of parties. He enjoyed wine and drinking. 'A life without festivity is a long road without an inn,' he wrote. His occasional frivolities weren't a rejection of his more serious insights and tasks. They were what kept up his spirits so that he could continue to engage with the difficulties of life – and therefore, though they might not have been serious in themselves, they had an extremely serious role to play in the overall economy of his existence. Democritus did not believe that he had to feel constantly sad to prove that he recognised life to be sad. He danced every now and then because of a rightful confidence that he had already done justice – and would always in the future fully do justice – to the sadness of things.

Evoke for yourself a series of reasons why it might be wholly legitimate to despair – but also to remain cheerful.

Reasons to despair	Reasons to be cheerful

Once we have acquired the skill of Cheerful Despair, a new range of possibilities for pleasure opens itself up to us. We will be amazed and so touched when, once in a while, someone seems to understand a few things we mean. We will take note, with some astonishment, that not everyone has plans to murder or hurt others. We will make the most of the constrained but real opportunities we have. We will be free to enjoy the distinctive Cheerful Despair of those who have taken every fateful fact about life on board – and yet smile.

Image Credits

p. 11
Pieter Brueghel the Elder, *The Dutch Proverbs*, 1559. Oil on oak wood, 117.2 cm × 163.8 cm. Gemäldegalerie, Berlin, Germany / Wikimedia Commons

p. 23 [top]
sangsiripech / Shutterstock

p. 23 [bottom]
Brian Gratwicke / Flickr (CC BY 2.0)

p. 26 [top]
Rogier van der Weyden, *The Magdalen Reading*, c. 1438. Oil on mahogany, transferred from another panel, 62.2 cm × 54.4 cm. National Gallery, London, England / Wikimedia Commons

p. 26 [bottom]
Giovanni Bellini, *Madonna and Child with Saints Catherine and Mary Magdalene [detail]*, c. 1490. Oil on panel, 58 cm × 107 cm. Gallerie dell 'Accademia, Venice. © José Luiz Bernardes Ribeiro / Wikimedia Commons (CC BY-SA 4.0)

p. 29
Portrait of M. Klein, half-length, seated, 1957. Wellcome Collection / Wikimedia Commons

p. 30
Engin Akyurt / Unsplash

p. 35 [top]
Sèvres Porcelain Bleu Celeste '1867 Exhibition' vases and covers, 1860. 1stdibs

p. 35 [bottom]
Unknown Dosai or Doraku artist, Japan, Edo period, 19th century. Raku-type clay with Black Raku glaze, gold lacquer repairs, 13.4 cm × 12 cm. Freer Gallery of Art, Smithsonian Institution, Washington, D.C.: USA. Gift of Charles Lang Freer, F1894.16

p. 68
Lebrecht Music & Arts / Alamy Stock Photo

p. 69 [top]
Gilt-bronze Seated Amitabha Buddha, Joseon Dynasty (1392–1897), H 27.9 cm. National Museum of Korea, Seoul, South Korea / Wikimedia Commons

p. 69 [bottom]
'Pseudo-Seneca' marble bust of Seneca, 2nd century BCE. British Museum, London, England. Marie-Lan Nguyen / Wikimedia Commons

p. 71
Manuel Domínguez Sánchez, *The Death of Seneca*, 1871. Oil on canvas, 270 cm × 450 cm. Museo Nacional del Prado, Madrid, Spain / Wikimedia Commons

p. 74
Caspar David Friedrich, *Reefs by the Seashore*, 1824. Oil on canvas, 22 cm × 31 cm. Staatliche Kunsthalle (State Art Gallery), Karlsruhe, Germany / Wikimedia Commons

p. 76
ESA / Hubble and NASA / Wikimedia Commons

p. 78
Hiroshi Sugimoto, *North Atlantic Ocean, Cliffs of Moher*, 1989. Gelatin silver print, 38.8 × 58.4 cm. Courtesy of the artist and Marian Goodman Gallery. © Hiroshi Sugimoto

p. 96
"Archaic Torso of Apollo," translation copyright © 1982 by Stephen Mitchell; from *Selected Poetry of Rainer Maria Rilke* by Rainer Maria Rilke, edited and translated by Stephen Mitchell. Used by permission of Random House, an imprint and division of Penguin Random House LLC. All rights reserved.

p. 110
Claude Lorraine, *Landscape with Hagar and the Angel*, 1646. Oil on canvas mounted on wood, 52.2 cm × 42.3 cm. National Gallery, London, England. Presented by Sir George Beaumont, 1828 / Wikimedia Commons

p. 111
Georges Braque, *Nature Morte (Fruit Dish, Ace of Clubs)*, 1913. Oil, gouache and charcoal on canvas, 81 cm × 60 cm, Musée National d'Art Moderne, Centre Georges Pompidou, Paris, France. / Wikimedia Commons. © ADAGP, Paris and DACS, London 2021

p. 117
John Stuart Mill, c. 1870. London Stereoscopic Company / Hulton Archive / Wikimedia Commons

p. 118
Abbus Acastra / Alamy Stock Photo

p. 120
Fashion Plate (London Fashionable Walking Dresses) from *The Lady's Magazine*, 1812. Hand-colored engraving on paper. Los Angeles County Museum of Art, Los Angeles, USA. Gift of Dr. and Mrs. Gerald Labiner (M.86.266.104) / Wikimedia Commons

p. 124 [top]
Keystone Press / Alamy Stock Photo

p. 124 [bottom]
Ian Kelsall / Unsplash

p. 127
Eric Fidler / Flickr (CC BY-NC 2.0)

p. 143
Dr Mourad Boudiaf / ISM / Science Photo Library

p. 144
Niclas Moser / Unsplash

p. 187
Peter Paul Rubens, *Heraclitus and Democritus*, 1603. Oil on canvas, 95 cm × 125 cm. Museo Nacional de Escultura, Valladolid, Spain / Wikimedia Commons

The School of Life is a global organisation helping people lead more fulfilled lives. It is a resource for helping us understand ourselves, for improving our relationships, our careers and our social lives – as well as for helping us find calm and get more out of our leisure hours. We do this through films, workshops, books, apps, gifts and community. You can find us online, in stores and in welcoming spaces around the globe.